The Parker Family Circus

A PLAY BY
Jan Buttram

SAMUEL FRENCH, INC.

45 West 25th Street   7623 Sunset Boulevard
NEW YORK 10010   HOLLYWOOD 90046
LONDON   *TORONTO*

Copyright © 2003 by Jan Buttram

ALL RIGHTS RESERVED

CAUTION: Professionals and amateurs are hereby warned that THE PARKER FAMILY CIRCUS is subject to a royalty. It is fully protected under the copyright laws of the United States of America, the British Commonwealth, including Canada, and all other countries of the Copyright Union. All rights, including professional, amateur, motion pictures, recitation, lecturing, public reading, radio broadcasting, television, and the rights of translation into foreign languages are strictly reserved. In its present form the play is dedicated to the reading public only.

The amateur live stage performance rights to THE PARKER FAMILY CIRCUS are controlled exclusively by Samuel French, Inc. and royalty arrangements and licenses must be secured well in advance of presentation. PLEASE NOTE that amateur royalty fees are set upon application in accordance with your producing circumstances. When applying for a royalty quotation and license please give us the number of performances intended, dates of production, your seating capacity and admission fee. Royalties are payable one week before the opening performance of the play to Samuel French, Inc., at 45 W. 25th Street, New York, NY 10010; or at 7623 Sunset Blvd., Hollywood, CA 90046, or to Samuel French (Canada), Ltd., 100 Lombard Street, Lower Level, Toronto, Ontario, Canada M5C 1M3.

Royalty of the required amount must be paid whether the play is presented for charity or gain and whether or not admission is charged.

Stock royalty quoted on application to Samuel French, Inc.

For all rights other than those stipulated above, apply to Fifi Oscard Agency, 110 W. 40th Street, Suite 1601, New York, NY 10018.

Particular emphasis is laid on the question of amateur or professional readings, permission and terms for which must be secured in writing from Samuel French, Inc.

Copying from this book in whole or in part is strictly forbidden by law, and the right of performance is not transferable.

Whenever the play is produced the following notice must appear on all programs, printing and advertising for the play: "Produced by special arrangement with Samuel French, Inc."

Due authorship credit must be given on all programs, printing and advertising for the play.

ISBN 0 573 62914 5   Printed in U.S.A.   #17822

No one shall commit or authorize any act or omission by which the copyright of, or the right to copyright, this play may be impaired.

No one shall make any changes in this play for the purpose of production.

Publication of this play does not imply availability for performance. Both amateurs and professionals considering a production are *strongly* advised in their own interests to apply to Samuel French, Inc., for written permission before starting rehearsals, advertising, or booking a theatre.

No part of this book may be reproduced, stored in a retrieval system, or transmitted in any form, by any means, now known or yet to be invented, including mechanical, electronic, photocopying, recording, videotaping, or otherwise, without the prior written permission of the publisher.

IMPORTANT BILLING AND CREDIT REQUIREMENTS

All producers of THE PARKER FAMILY CIRCUS *must* give credit to the Author of the Play in all programs distributed in connection with performances of the Play and in all instances in which the title of the Play appears for purposes of advertising, publicizing or otherwise exploiting the Play and/or a production. The name of the Author *must* also appear on a separate line, on which no other name appears, immediately following the title, and *must* appear in size of type not less than fifty percent the size of the title type.

A NOTE ON THE USE OF VIDEOTAPING

Videotaping may be granted to *amateur* productions under certain conditions and restrictions. Please contact Samuel French, Inc. for information.

*Premiere Performance at the Blue Heron Arts Center,
New York City: February 8, 2002*

Abingdon Theatre Company

Jan Buttram & Pamela Paul, *Artistic Directors*   Samuel J. Bellinger, *Managing Director*

presents

The Parker Family Circus

a new play by
Jan Buttram

Directed by Taylor Brooks

Cast

Pearl (Mamaw) Parker	Rita Gardner
Tommy Parker	Bryan Schany
Polly Parker	Lori Gardner
Vesta Moody	Debbie Jaffe
Lottie Parker	Carole Monferdini
Don Parker	Michael Pemberton

Scenic Design	*Production Stage Mgr.*	*Casting*
James F. Wolk	Eric Selk	Cindi Rush, C.S.A.
Lighting Design	*Assistant Director*	*Publicity*
David Castaneda	Jeff Silverman	Shirely Herz Assoc.
Costume Design	*Assistant Stage Mgr.*	*Graphic Design*
Ingrid Maurer	Stephanie Dodd	Anthony Rubolotta
Production Manager	*Dramaturg*	
Peter Brouwer	Julie Hegner	

Abington Theatre Company Workshop Production

Directed by Taylor Brooks

Cast

Pearl (Mamaw) Parker	Rita Gardner
Tommy Parker	Bryan Schany
Polly Parker	Lori Gardner
Vesta Moody	Debbie Jaffe
Lottie Parker	Carole Monferdini
Don Parker	David Newer

Set Design	*Lighting Design*	*Assistant Director*
Elizabeth Chaney	Kim T. Sharp	Alex Dery
Costume Design	*Production Stage Mgr.*	*Box Office Mgr.*
Ingrid Maurer	Ernie Delli Santi III	Jerry O'Connell

CHARACTERS

PEARL "MAMAW" PARKER: 72, the grandmother. She is friendly, good-natured and warm. She is a widow and grieving.

TOMMY PARKER: 20, the grandson. He has an I.Q. of 70 and is volatile, with the social maturity of an eight- or nine-year-old. He adores his grandmother.

POLLY PEARL PARKER: 16, the granddaughter. She is smart, pretty and popular. She has a terrific temper.

VESTA MOODY: 16, the family friend. She is cynical but friendly, from a broken home.

LOTTIE PARKER: 46, the mother. A high school guidance counselor, she is pretty, driven and competitive.

DON PARKER: 46: the son. A talented electrician, he is the production manager at the sports/performance arena. He is good-natured and loves his family, but he's confused by life.

TIME

The present

PLACE

Mamaw's living room in Plano, Texas

For Taylor Brooks

ACT I

(A living room with the entrance door up stage leading to a porch. The furniture is comfortable with an old console TV featured prominently. Papaw's chair, an easy chair with a matching ottoman, is worn and dark. Mamaw's rocker is smaller.
PEARL (MAMAW) PARKER, a handsome woman of 72, recovers her sofa with bright floral-patterned material. There is a distant shout.)

TOMMY. *(Offstage.)* STAY AWAY FROM ME! *(MAMAW goes to the door.)* DON'T COME OVER HERE!
MAMAW. Goodness!

(MAMAW opens the front door.)

TOMMY *(Offstage.)* Heh!!! Stay over there! I'm over here ... Don't come over HEREEEE!

(MAMAW shushes from the door.)

MAMAW. Tommy! Get in here! You heard me ... mind what I'm saying.

(TOMMY PARKER, twenty, a good-looking but slow-witted young man, is at the door yelling offstage)

TOMMY. I SEE YOU!
MAMAW. Stop yelling like that! You can't just stand in the driveway yelling. People will think you're simpleminded.

(TOMMY enters, scared. Embraces his grandmother.)

TOMMY. I got scared you wasn't here.
MAMAW. I'm here. You'll be twenty years old soon, hon'... act like it.
TOMMY. I'm not supposed to come inside if you're not here. I been standing out there for two hours.
MAMAW. Two hours! Did you get out of school early?
TOMMY. Some.
MAMAW. It's not polite to yell at people.
TOMMY. Why ain't the TV on? The TV is always on ... why ain't it on?

(MAMAW returns to her work. TOMMY sits in Papaw's chair, picks up the remote control. Clicks.)

MAMAW. Broke. *(He clicks several times, nothing.)* Tommy. It's broke. *(TOMMY jumps up and hits the television.)* Stop it, now.
TOMMY. What's wrong with it?
MAMAW. It quit.
TOMMY. When you going to get it fixed?
MAMAW. I might not get it fixed.
TOMMY. Why?
MAMAW. Might cost too much.
TOMMY. Shit.
MAMAW. Tommy. You know I'll not stand for cussing.
TOMMY. I've got to watch "Planet Xenon."
MAMAW. Do something else.
TOMMY. What?
MAMAW. I don't know. Read one of your funny books.
TOMMY. But it's time for "Planet Xenon." That's what I watch at 3:00. It's just trouble everywhere.
MAMAW. Hon', missing a cartoon show is not trouble.
TOMMY. Yes, it is.
MAMAW. Well, I'm sorry if you're upset.
TOMMY. What's going to happen to me?

MAMAW. Nothing.

(TOMMY sits back in Papaw's chair.)

TOMMY. Something bad. I'm not leaving this house ever again.

MAMAW. You'd get mighty bored. Why is something bad going to happen?

TOMMY. If Papaw was here, he could fix the TV.

MAMAW. Your granddaddy could fix any TV made. He and your daddy and your Uncle Cory, why, they'd work all night back in the shop, fixing somebody's TV or lawn mower.

TOMMY. Fixing everybody's stuff.

MAMAW. Why, you couldn't get 'em to quit and go to bed. Just sometimes in the summer, they'd quit early and Papaw and me would sit on the porch and watch those boys roll around the yard like a couple of puppies, giggling and whispering and wrestling. They'd gnaw each other to pieces.

TOMMY. The Parker Family Circus.

MAMAW. That's what Papaw called it.

TOMMY. Nothing's any good since Papaw died.

MAMAW. That's not true. Watching you out in the driveway just now, the back of your head reminded me of Papaw.

TOMMY. It did?

MAMAW. Every night he'd walk up that driveway carrying his lunch box.

TOMMY. I remember that lunch box.

MAMAW. I always had him a good lunch.

TOMMY. Mamaw ... I remember something! I remember!

MAMAW. What, hon'?

TOMMY. Papaw brought home Birddog in his lunch box.

MAMAW. Yes, he did. Papaw would be wore out but he'd see me waving and his eyes would perk up.

TOMMY. He was glad to see you.

MAMAW. Course, the reality of Papaw walking through the door never lived up to the expectation of his walking up the driveway.

TOMMY. How come?

MAMAW. Just never did. He'd unlace those old steel-toe boots and holler, "Oh, thank you, Jesus."

TOMMY. You could kick butt with steel in your shoes.

MAMAW. Them shoes weren't for kicking butt. They were to protect a fellow's toe if a helicopter engine come crashing down. He like to got hurt bad once or twice.

TOMMY. He was safe when he got here in this house. Like Ramona the Revenger—no one can touch her when she gets inside her rocket ship.

MAMAW. Papaw would lean back in his chair and give a big sigh and say, "Mama, I sure am glad to be home."

TOMMY. And you'd say ...

MAMAW. "I'm glad to have you home."

TOMMY. And now it's me, you're glad to see me.

(MAMAW hugs TOMMY.)

MAMAW. I sure am.

TOMMY. And I'm safe when I get here, just like Papaw.

MAMAW. You're always welcome here.

TOMMY. Mamaw, I ain't never going back to that school. The kids, the teachers, they all call me names. They think I'm dumb.

MAMAW. Kids can be mean.

TOMMY. Mamaw, I'm coming to live with you.

(MAMAW returns to recovering her sofa.)

MAMAW. Your momma would miss you.

TOMMY. Nuh unh.

MAMAW. And your daddy ....

TOMMY. Daddy's just a mean son-of-a-bitch.

MAMAW. Tommy, hush.

TOMMY. Papaw said daddy was the meanest man he ever knew.

MAMAW. He ought not have.

TOMMY. Daddy turned Uncle Cory over to the law, cause he was so mean.

MAMAW. What are you talking about?

TOMMY. Daddy turned his own brother over to the sheriff for stealing.

MAMAW. That's a terribly wrong-headed idea, hon'. You can't just make things up like that!

TOMMY. Papaw told me. Daddy told the law that Uncle Cory was a damn thief and told 'em where to find him to put him in the cuffs.

MAMAW. Listen here, hon', Uncle Cory turned himself in. Your daddy didn't have a thing to do ….

TOMMY. Nuh unh ….

MAMAW. Don't contradict me!

TOMMY. Papaw said to keep it a secret. I swore a blood oath not to tell and I never did—not while he was alive.

MAMAW. Tommy. Now. Your grandfather liked to spin tales.

(TOMMY paces.)

TOMMY. Everything Papaw said was true. Papaw was the only one I could talk to, I could tell him anything. He didn't think I was simpleminded. And Papaw wouldn't like what you're doing to his couch.

MAMAW. Well, I didn't like him burning cigarette holes in all my furniture, neither.

TOMMY. Papaw wouldn't let the TV get broke.

MAMAW. Leaving it on day and night, no wonder it just quit. This morning, I could hear birds singing. That was a change.

TOMMY. Papaw wouldn't yell at me.

MAMAW. Hon', your granddaddy is gone, nigh six months.

TOMMY. What's going to happen to me?

MAMAW. Now, hon', I know life is painful sometimes. But that's when we have to put our faith in the good Lord and be brave. And I'm here for you and your mother, and your daddy ….

TOMMY. Momma's going to turn me into the law.

(MAMAW goes to TOMMY.)

MAMAW. Why? Did you do something bad?

(After a beat, TOMMY caresses his grandmother's shoulders.)

TOMMY. You want me to rub your shoulders?
MAMAW. No, thank you.
TOMMY. Why not?
MAMAW. My arthritis doesn't hurt a bit today, thank the Lord.

(MAMAW returns to her work. TOMMY paces.)

TOMMY. I got to find a girlfriend.
MAMAW. Well, you will.
TOMMY. I need a girlfriend bad.
MAMAW. Be patient. Where's your sister?
TOMMY. Polly don't care about nothing but getting to be governor of Texas or President of the world, like she has a chance.
MAMAW. Your sister tries for a lot.
TOMMY. Polly's always running around with Vesta. They're like glued together.
MAMAW. That's how young girls do.
TOMMY. Vesta and Polly are lesbians.
MAMAW. Now, son, that's just too much. I'm going to throw my shoe at you.
TOMMY. They are always sitting on top of each other.
MAMAW. When's your momma coming in?
TOMMY. Momma's telling everyone in Plano, Texas, what to do. Selling houses, driving around the streets searching for men.
MAMAW. Tommy, stop acting up.
TOMMY. Sellin' our house for a lot of money. Mamaw, you've got to—you've just got to help me. If you don't, I'm going to just blow up.
MAMAW. What in kingdom come happened today?
TOMMY. Everything in my life happened.
MAMAW. Yes, but exactly what?
TOMMY. My L - I - F - E.
MAMAW. What in your L - I - F - E?
TOMMY. Where I go to school. Where I live. My brain. My

body. It's all happening wrong.

(TOMMY bursts into tears, sits on the sofa. MAMAW moves to comfort him.)

MAMAW. I'll do anything I can to help you, hon'. *(He throws his arms around her and she pats and rocks him. His crying stops. His hands move under her clothes. She pulls away.)* Watch your hands, son! Never touch a woman in a personal place 'less she gives her permission. *(TOMMY grins sheepishly.)* My goodness.
TOMMY. I love you. Do you love me?

(MAMAW tries to recover. She exits to the kitchen.)

MAMAW. I figured y'all would come in hungry. I've been baking ... and there's black-eyed peas and some sweet potato casserole.

(Sounds of girls giggling on the porch. TOMMY races to the door. Yells out.)

TOMMY. Shit! I told you not to come over here!

(POLLY, Tommy's sister, and VESTA, her best friend, both 16, enter as TOMMY exits to the bedroom. POLLY follows.)

POLLY. Tommy Parker, come back here! You've ruined my life!

(VESTA has several body piercings. She eats a bag of potato chips, crumbs fall. Clicks the remote. Nothing. MAMAW enters.)

MAMAW. Vesta, watch those chips, hon'. I've got new slipcovers.
VESTA. Sorry.
MAMAW. And you're sitting on straight pins.... *(VESTA is not concerned.)* How are you?
VESTA. I'm OK.

MAMAW. Tommy is awful upset.
VESTA. Well, it was a weird day.
MAMAW. In what way?
VESTA. Just weird.

(MAMAW sits in Papaw's chair.)

MAMAW. Tommy got out early?
VESTA. Uh huh.
MAMAW. Special occasion?
VESTA. Naw.
MAMAW. Everyone didn't get out?
VESTA. Naw.
MAMAW. Did Tommy get into some trouble?
VESTA. He's always in trouble 'cause he's slow and kids make fun. You know. But today was a new level of bizarre.
MAMAW. Hon', I'll give you something better than those potato chips….
VESTA. Do you have Crispy Creme doughnuts?
MAMAW. No. Sit over here hon'.

(VESTA moves to Papaw's chair.)

VESTA. What's wrong with your TV?
MAMAW. Can't say.
VESTA. What will you do?

(MAMAW sits on the sofa, clearing potato chip residue.)

MAMAW. I don't know. Let you kids entertain me.
VESTA. Huh?

(A door slams. POLLY yells out.)

POLLY. *(Offstage.)* TOMMY! LET ME IN THERE!
MAMAW. How is your daddy?

THE PARKER FAMILY CIRCUS 15

VESTA. My daddy?
MAMAW. Yes.
VESTA. Are you asking about my daddy or the stepdaddy I have now?
MAMAW. Your real daddy, hon'.
VESTA. Carl Moody is my daddy. But ....
MAMAW. Carl is who I'm asking about. You favor him.
VESTA. I do?
MAMAW. Around the eyes.
POLLY. *(Offstage.)* You're such a BUTTHOLE!
TOMMY. *(Offstage.)* SHUT UP! SHUT UP! SHUT UP!
POLLY. *(Offstage.)* I WILL NEVER FORGIVE YOU! NEVER!

(A door slams. MAMAW goes to the door.)

MAMAW. Polly! Leave your brother alone.... *(MAMAW returns to VESTA.)* Are you going to make a lawyer like your daddy did?
VESTA. I'm sixteen years old. I haven't a clue what I'm going to do.
MAMAW. Sometimes folks want their kids to go do like they did.
VESTA. I will not go do like my daddy or go do like my stepdaddy. I will not be a lawyer and I will not sell cars.
MAMAW. Not too many women car salesmen anyhow.
VESTA. For good reason. *(VESTA gets a call on her cellular.)* Heh. No. No. I'll try. OK.

(VESTA hangs up.)

MAMAW. Are those cell phones expensive?
VESTA. Yeah. Mom works for the Southwestern Bell so ....
MAMAW. She gets a bargain.
VESTA. I suppose.
MAMAW. I may buy one myself. You'd have to teach me how to use it.
VESTA. Cool.

MAMAW. I'm taking a trip. There may not be a lot of phones in Nicaragua.
VESTA. Central America?
MAMAW. That's right.
VESTA. Whoa.
MAMAW. I'm still in the planning.
VESTA. Massive.
MAMAW. I was thinking about your granddaddy, now that his wife is passed on, we're both widowed ... he might want to travel some….
VESTA. Which granddaddy?
MAMAW. Mr. Moody ... Parnel Moody.
VESTA. He's dead.
MAMAW. Law. When?
VESTA. Oh, I don't know ... a while.

(POLLY enters.)

POLLY. Mamaw, make him do right!
MAMAW. Now, hon', can't y'all be nice to one another?
POLLY. You just don't understand! *(She exits, yelling.)* TOMMY!!!!
MAMAW. What in the world ....
VESTA. I don't get involved.
MAMAW. Parnel and I had the same birthday. September 14th. Your granddaddy courted me once.
VESTA. What did you do, blow him off or something?
MAMAW. Oh no. We churned homemade ice cream.

(POLLY runs in holding a stack of comic books. TOMMY chases her, furious.)

TOMMY. Give me my funny books!
MAMAW. Polly, now, stop teasing him!
POLLY. You listen to me or I'll never give them to you!
TOMMY. Give 'em now!

(POLLY exits to the bedrooms. TOMMY follows. Door slams. MAMAW follows them to the door.)

MAMAW. Stop slamming my doors!
VESTA. *(Intrigued.)* How do you churn something?

(MAMAW returns to recovering her sofa.)

MAMAW. Well, you take whatever you're churning and move a stick or whatever back and forth and up and down or around.
VESTA. And it makes ice cream.
MAMAW. Oh, yes. Very good ice cream.
VESTA. Why wouldn't you just buy it?
TOMMY. *(Offstage.)* Polly!
MAMAW. It's better homemade.
VESTA. So, you'd, like, *churn* it.
MAMAW. You took an iron freezer and put in the makings, then you put that freezer part in the middle of this larger wooden bucket, and put ice and rock salt in the space in between.
VESTA. Sounds way complicated.
MAMAW. Well, it was an event. Your real daddy might remember doing it.
VESTA. Maybe. He's pretty old.
TOMMY. *(Offstage.)* Polly! Give 'em back!!!!
POLLY. *(Offstage.)* NO!

(Door slam.)

MAMAW. If I hear anymore, I'm calling your mother!
VESTA. Like what are makings?
MAMAW. Sugar, milk, and fresh fruit. You churn makings and it turns into ice cream. Course, you'd need a person to sit on the whole thing while another person cranked the freezer so the insides turned round 'n round and the ice cream would freeze. That day your granddad cranked and I sat on the freezer ....
VESTA. Uh huh.

MAMAW. Well, I sat and sat and he cranked and cranked and nothing was happening because it didn't get harder for him to crank ....

VESTA. Uh huh.

MAMAW. Then I remembered what I forgot. *(Beat.)* I had forgot to put in sweet milk.

VESTA. Milk?

MAMAW. I'd just put in the peaches and the sugar but I hadn't put in the rest of the makings.

VESTA. So, you, like, had to tell him?

MAMAW. Well, I was just about your age and I didn't tell. I just let him keep cranking. And when he was a puddle of sweat because it was fire-popping hot, he said, "Get off of that freezer, Pearl." I did, and he pulled the top off and looked inside, and there was nothing but peaches and sugar. He got up and walked off and never spoke to me again. He was a very nice-looking boy.

VESTA. Now that he's dead, I'm down to six grandparents instead of seven.

MAMAW. Well, isn't that interesting.

VESTA. Connie Watson holds the record for having the most grandparents. She has like twelve grandparents. But I might as well not have the new grandparents because they live in Chicago. They think we're hillbillies. My third grandmother was living with us but my little brother was running through the house and tripped her and she broke her hip.

MAMAW. Oh, Lord.

VESTA. He's so dumb. He's not as dumb as Tommy but still ....

MAMAW. Don't say dumb, hon'. Tommy's just simpleminded. *(VESTA has no comment.)* Do you like my slip covers?

VESTA. They're OK.

MAMAW. I think they'll turn out pretty.

VESTA. This house is cool. It's not like "Plano Clinique."

MAMAW. My daddy built this house. I've had many offers to sell it.

VESTA. They'd tear it down.

MAMAW. This was all countryside. Very few houses.

VESTA. Now it's just snob city.

MAMAW. Nobody waves at you anymore. Used to, everyone waved when they saw you driving down the street or standing in your yard....

VESTA. Wow. Heh, Mrs. Parker. Tommy told some kids he was going to sell his comic books.

MAMAW. Is that a fact?

VESTA. He's got some real old ones. They're worth a bunch of money.

POLLY. *(Offstage.)* TAKE THEM! JERK!

TOMMY. *(Offstage.)* LEAVE ME ALONE!!!

(Door slam.)

MAMAW. Did he ask some girl to have sex with him again?

VESTA. Tandy Woo is such a slut. She's screaming, "Get out of my face, you jerk off, or I'll sue you for sexual harassment." And she caught like a case of syphilis last year so Tommy's lucky she wouldn't do it with him.

(POLLY enters and sits on VESTA's lap.)

MAMAW. Sit on a chair, hon'.

POLLY. Are we eating supper here?

MAMAW. I don't rightly know. Be good to your brother, Polly, he's having a hard time.

POLLY. He's always having a hard time. He's had a hard time every milli-second of my life. I wish they'd just send me to private school. Vesta's mother is sending her to Austin.

MAMAW. Why, Vesta, don't you want to finish out where you started?

VESTA. I don't care. They've got this thing about it.

POLLY. She is so lucky. I'm so nervous. My head is itching.

MAMAW. Well, what happened?

POLLY. Mamaw, I can't even tell you. It's too horrendous.

VESTA. She's freaked.

MAMAW. And I haven't been much help to you lately.
VESTA. She's all scared you're going to die.
POLLY. I am not!
VESTA. It's what you said.
POLLY. I never did.
VESTA. You most certainly did. You were, like, crying and stuff.
POLLY. Will you, like, shut your big fat mouth!
VESTA. Oh, please. You were hysterical.
POLLY. You are so like "the voice of Plano."
MAMAW. Polly?
POLLY. Well, Daddy was the one that said it.
MAMAW. Said what?
POLLY. He said you'll die from missing Papaw.
MAMAW. I will not.
POLLY. Because your mother died three months after your daddy died.
MAMAW. What does that have to do with it?
POLLY. Mother said it could happen because your identity as a person was all wrapped up in Papaw.
MAMAW. That's pure nonsense.
POLLY. Mamaw, like, you've got to promise me you won't say anything to Daddy. He'll know I told you.
MAMAW. Lucky for you, I'm leaving soon.
POLLY. To go where?
MAMAW. My church group is fixing to rebuild an orphanage in Nicaragua.
POLLY. Mamaw!
MAMAW. Don't you tell.
POLLY. If you promise not to tell Daddy I repeated him. I hate it when he's mad at me.
MAMAW. All right.

(Checking her watch, POLLY is up, kissing her grandmother.)

POLLY. Whoa! Got to go.
MAMAW. Lot's up?

POLLY. Student council.

VESTA. Thrilling. Bye, Mrs. Parker.

MAMAW. Bye. *(They exit. A beat. TOMMY enters, carrying the stack of funny books. He plops down in Papaw's chair, counting his comics. MAMAW begins putting away her sewing materials.)* You want to talk about it?

TOMMY. Naw, I'll just let everyone else tell you.

MAMAW. If you let everyone else tell it, I might not get the right story.

TOMMY. I don't care.

MAMAW. Did you tell your mother you left school early?

TOMMY. She's just a big mouth. I hate her.

MAMAW. You do not hate your mother.

TOMMY. Everybody better leave me alone.

MAMAW. Who's everybody?

TOMMY. Just everybody. *(MAMAW exits. TOMMY imitates an Indian on the warpath, hopping up and down. MAMAW returns with a damp cloth and spot cleans her slipcovers)* Long time back, there was some Indian tribe that drank their own piss.

MAMAW. I didn't know that.

TOMMY. They did it to make themselves strong. I drank some of mine.

MAMAW. Oh, please, son.

TOMMY. I want to get strong ... random annihilation.

MAMAW. Who was you planning to annihilate?

TOMMY. Anyone who looks at me. Ramona punctures the eyes of her enemies and drives steel spikes through their brains ....

MAMAW. You might as well spit it out. I'm going to hear it sooner or later.

(TOMMY sits in Papaw's chair.)

TOMMY. Last week, I heard Sonny Riggins ask Tandy Woo to have sex with him and she laughed at him and said she'd have to check her date book, she had a busy day.

MAMAW. Law, I never.

TOMMY. So when I asked her the same thing, she 'bout took my head off.
MAMAW. Is that what happened? Well, neither one of you was acting right.
TOMMY. Everyone has a girlfriend but me. You had Papaw.
MAMAW. Hon', I was more than his girlfriend.
TOMMY. I like Papaw's chair.
MAMAW. It's a good one.
TOMMY. And you give me his hunting jacket.
MAMAW. Lots of wear left.
TOMMY. You said it looks like it belongs on me.
MAMAW. It does.
TOMMY. Papaw smoked cigarettes. He told me he'd take me out and shoot me if I smoked cigarettes so I ain't gonna.
MAMAW. Now, that's smart thinking, Tommy.

(TOMMY giggles, pleased.)

TOMMY. You think I'm smart.
MAMAW. I do when you talk like that. I think you're real smart.
TOMMY. I've got a good idea. *(He flirts with his grandmother.)* I've thought about it a long time and I think it makes a lot of sense.

(MAMAW sits on the sofa.)

MAMAW. Well, let's hear it.
TOMMY. You can be my girlfriend.
MAMAW. Come again?
TOMMY. Be my girlfriend? You're the prettiest girl I know.
MAMAW. I'm not understanding you.
TOMMY. I have to get someone to have sex with. Could you and me have sex?
MAMAW. I'm your grandmother.
TOMMY. That don't make no difference.

(MAMAW rises, angry. He follows her.)

MAMAW. I oughta slap your face off.

TOMMY. You said you thought I was smart.

MAMAW. Hon', are you trying to shock me?

TOMMY. Mamaw, nobody will be my girlfriend. They're all doin' it with someone. I want to do it, too.

MAMAW. I can't put up with this. I'm an old woman.

TOMMY. How old?

MAMAW. Seventy-two years.

TOMMY. That's not old.

MAMAW. It's wrong. It's plain wrong.

TOMMY. Nuh un...

MAMAW. When have I ever given you cause to talk to me like this? The good Lord does not have such things in mind as what you're thinking.

TOMMY. I don't believe some old man is sitting up there making us do things. And he ain't a good person or he wouldn't just bury zillions of people alive or drown 'em or blow 'em up.

MAMAW. What people are you talking about?

TOMMY. All over Plano and New York City—everywhere else, zillions and zillions—random annihilation.

(LOTTIE, Tommy's mother, enters. She is a good-looking woman of 45, dressed simply but upscale. Beautiful scarf. TOMMY exits, quickly.)

LOTTIE. I'd beat it outta here, too, young man. *(A door slams. LOTTIE follows. OFFSTAGE yelling.)* Lock yourself in the bathroom! You're going to get mighty bored in there. I don't know, Tommy. I just don't know how long we're supposed to watch this trauma drama. *(Re-enters the living room. Seeing MAMAW.)* Mamaw, you're flushed ....

MAMAW. Am I? I was cooking and it's ... hot in the kitchen. That is a beautiful scarf, Lottie. I've not seen it before.

LOTTIE. A present from the senior class. I'm just checking in ....

(MAMAW sits in her rocker.)

MAMAW. I was just about to call you. Take Tommy home.
LOTTIE. Why?
MAMAW. He needs to go home.

(LOTTIE begins to exit the house)

LOTTIE. Mamaw, he can't go home. There's no one there... 8:00 latest ....
MAMAW. I won't be here.

(LOTTIE returns.)

LOTTIE. Where will you be?
MAMAW. I have to be somewhere.
LOTTIE. You didn't tell me.
MAMAW. He's real upset.
LOTTIE. I've got to be places. Did he tell you what happened at school?
MAMAW. Yes.
LOTTIE. All of it?
MAMAW. Enough.
LOTTIE. So you're saying he can't stay here?
MAMAW. That's what I'm saying.
LOTTIE. I depend on you. He always comes here.
MAMAW. Well, not today. Take him with you.
LOTTIE. Mamaw, I can't take him with me and I can't leave him alone.
MAMAW. Lottie, take him.
LOTTIE. We'll see about this.

(LOTTIE sits on the ottoman, dials her cell phone. The line is busy. She continues to redial during the next scene.)

MAMAW. I'm sorry. I feel for him, of course. He was sitting right here and Papaw just keeled over.
LOTTIE. Mamaw, my son is about to cost me my job. *(On the*

phone.) Call me!

MAMAW. Your teaching?

LOTTIE. We're in a zero tolerance zone—kids do not act out in the Plano school district. This new principal watches me like a hawk. He wasn't around when I brought this school through the suicide epidemic of '99, not to mention the heroin trafficking scandal. All he sees is three cheerleaders who managed to get themselves knocked up. That little creep actually suggested I transfer Tommy to Denton State School. My son in that vegetable bin? I didn't blink. I looked him straight in the eye and said, "Tommy has an I.Q. of 70. He is slow, *not* retarded." And now, because I refuse to bow down in front of the little jackass and say, "Thank you, thank you for your astounding advice," he has a stockpile of ammunition which he'll take to the school board and they'll transfer me to Siberia. He probably has some second cousin primed to take my job.

MAMAW. I think I might have to rest my eyes. I'm not feeling right.

LOTTIE. Did you call a doctor?

MAMAW. So, if y'all could go on, now.

LOTTIE. I'm spent. I truly am spent. All the kids at school, I help each and every one. I really make a difference and when it comes to my son, I'm no help whatsoever.

MAMAW. Well, he's missing Papaw.

LOTTIE. *(Dialing again.)* Where is everyone? It's so quiet in here. *(LOTTIE tries to turn on the TV.)* TV's dead?

MAMAW. Broke.

LOTTIE. Did you call someone?

MAMAW. No.

LOTTIE. Grief.

(LOTTIE paces the room, dialing.)

MAMAW. Papaw was sitting with Tommy, laughing and reading them funny books. I was putting in a new zipper on Papaw's trousers and Papaw starts coughing, then choking and grabbing his chest—then falls to the floor.

LOTTIE. Mamaw, you've told me this countless times.
MAMAW. Well, I'm just reminding you of the horror.

(MAMAW returns to clearing up her work on the sofa.)

LOTTIE. I am besieged with the bureaucracy of the public school system. I have hemorrhoids brought on by the frustration of trying to herd a bunch of wild cats ....

(LOTTIE dials again.)

MAMAW. There's the phone in the kitchen.
LOTTIE. It's a rotary, Mamaw. For the love of ... I bought you a new one.
MAMAW. I know.
LOTTIE. *(On the phone.)* Finally. Where are you?
MAMAW. Papaw didn't like that push button phone.
LOTTIE. What are you doing in Plano? ... Come to your mother's, please. *(Turning off the phone.)* Mamaw. Papaw's gone, now you can move into the modern age and throw out your rotary phone. You're working on new slip covers ... very pretty.

(She dials again.)

MAMAW. Well, the TV weren't working.

(LOTTIE sits in Mamaw's rocker.)

LOTTIE. *(Into the phone.)* Marie? Lottie Parker, I've hit a scheduling snag. Tomorrow? Ooh, lovely, I'm green. No, tonight isn't good. I'm due at a SWIP meeting ... "Students With Incarcerated Parents." I can't do real estate on school time. The eyes of Texas are upon me. But, listen, I just got a bead on a sweet Colonial for 1.5 over on Cherry Drive with almost an acre, guest cottage out back—beautiful pines, cedars, oaks—oh, it's pristine—four bedrooms, three baths, huge sundeck and screened porch with ceiling fans, stone terrace, wet bar, hot tub 18 by 36 ... nasty divorce—something about the hot tub and the babysitter. My client would go down, one million, cash. The stone terrace is made out of stone ... rocks.... I'll hold. That terrace will last longer than her new husband. It's too much money, she's got two kids at A&M—you know, I should show her our house...

(MAMAW straightens her sofa slipcover. She punctures her finger with a pin.)

MAMAW. Ouch.
LOTTIE. You could hire someone to do that.
MAMAW. They'd charge way too much. I thought you'd sold your house.
LOTTIE. It fell through.
MAMAW. Well, Lottie?
LOTTIE. Financing ... fell through.
MAMAW. I never understood why you would sell your home before the one you were building was ready ....
LOTTIE. The first rule of real estate, sell before you buy....
MAMAW. But you started building before you sold ....
LOTTIE. Well, I guess I didn't do it right then, did I?
MAMAW. Well, Law ....
LOTTIE. And the new house is way behind. We can't move until summer.
MAMAW. Summer?
LOTTIE. Mamaw. They lost the work permit—had to stop.
MAMAW. Stop work?
LOTTIE. Building code violation. I should sue this builder.
MAMAW. You need a permit to work?
LOTTIE. It's very complicated.
MAMAW. You're lucky those folks who bought it couldn't get their money together. You wouldn't have a place to live.
LOTTIE. We're coming to live with you.

(MAMAW sticks her finger again.)

MAMAW. Ouch!

LOTTIE. You and Papaw always said, "Come live with us. Your kids are over here most the time anyway." Course, I'd need to turn the bedroom closets into half-baths, we need a minimum of five bathrooms to sustain life on this planet .... *(On the phone.)* Hi, where are you? Really, if you've got two seconds ... in a lower price range, I'm selling my house for 250 thousand.... Oh, you hear every bit of news, don't you—the upstairs water damage is minor. We'll fix that in a jiffy IF you're truly interested. School's two blocks away. Yes, Tommy Parker is my son. They will not fire me. I've got tenure.

MAMAW. Oh, dear Lord, have mercy.

LOTTIE. I'm just across the street. I could show it to you real quick and if we're still talking, your husband can come over later, say eight o'clock? Take your call ... I'll wait. *(On hold. Calls out.)* Tommy, Daddy is coming here to take you with him so get ready. *(To MAMAW.)* OK? OK, let's see here. Your son, the love of my life, is seeing another woman. My mother is in a $1,000-a-day nursing home and doesn't recognize her only living daughter, my son can't be among civilized humans ... how was your day?

MAMAW. Lottie ....

LOTTIE. As usual, my husband is loading in a major show at the arena. Thank God he does not have to be held accountable for Tommy's antisocial behavior, his job is secure whereas mine .... *(Still on the cellular phone, she takes out a cigarette and crosses to the window.)* Well, you are something. No. I see you! No, no ... that's fine ... pull on into the driveway ... that's perfect.... *(Crosses to the hallway.)* Tommy, stay here! You move out of this house and I will personally execute you. I'm serious, Mamaw, he can't leave here. Don is on his way and I'll be back in a second.

(LOTTIE exits.)

MAMAW. I can't tell her.

(TOMMY enters carrying his comic books.)

TOMMY. She's nuts.
MAMAW. It's not polite to eavesdrop.

(He looks out window.)

TOMMY. She ain't movin' in here. This is my house. Papaw said it was mine.
MAMAW. Tommy. Quit acting bad.
TOMMY. Mamaw, don't you love me?
MAMAW. You're my grandson ... of course I love you.
TOMMY. You and me, we'll be girlfriend and boyfriend.
MAMAW. My Lord in heaven ... this would break your mother's heart....
TOMMY. We won't tell her. We'll be best friends, only friend we'll ever need. We'll read funny books and have sex all the time.
MAMAW. This is my fault. All my fault! *(She exits to the kitchen. TOMMY follows. She turns on him, furious.)* Tommy! Don't follow me!

(TOMMY, cowed, retreats to Papaw's chair. A beat. His mouth falls open, he grabs his chest, stands straight up and falls to the floor. Gets up. Goes through the ritual of Papaw's death again. VESTA and POLLY enter. TOMMY is on the floor.)

POLLY. Tommy ... *(He rises.)* You are such an asshole! What are you doing? *(Pushing TOMMY.)* They ... threw me off ... student council!
TOMMY. *(To VESTA.)* You got potato chips all over Mamaw's couch.
VESTA. Sorry.

(TOMMY pushes his sister back, she falls on the sofa. She is up in a flash, tackles her brother.)

POLLY. You butthole, butthole, butthole ....
VESTA. Stop it!

(VESTA pulls POLLY off TOMMY. POLLY and VESTA wrestle.)

    POLLY. Why are you fighting me?
    VESTA. You're just too brutal to him. You're, like, frightening.
    POLLY. You're the one that's frightening!

(MAMAW enters.)

    MAMAW. Stop yelling! Yelling around here, I've not had so much yelling in this house ever. Just quit it! You hear me? *(The girls settle a bit.)* Vesta, you got potato chips on the couch. That oil stain won't come out.

(MAMAW exits.)

    VESTA. Stressed.

(TOMMY gathers his comic books and crawls into Papaw's chair.)

    POLLY. I swear, you're my brother and all, but either Mother and Daddy do something or I'm liable to hit you on the head with Mamaw's iron skillet and risk getting the lethal injection. You bring it all on yourself. Lots of the kids have trouble learning but they don't make a federal case out of it. You won't let anyone help you.
    TOMMY. I don't want any help!
    POLLY. All right. Then I give up on you from here out! I mean, you hate Momma. You thought Papaw was God but he died so, surprise, he's not God. And every time I get to do something good, you screw it up.
    VESTA. Bad publicity is better than no publicity at all.
    POLLY. Shut your stupid face!
    VESTA. Excuse me? Every great politician has scuzzy relatives.
    POLLY. I can't believe you're going to sit there and belittle the fact that my life has been totaled by my brother—I'm trying to do something here…. You know, both of you just bring me down.

(POLLY exits to the bedroom.)

> VESTA. We worked really hard to get her elected to council.
> TOMMY. She's nuts.
> VESTA. So are you.

(POLLY enters, walks straight through the room, calling.)

> POLLY. MAMAW! Did I leave my cellular here?

(POLLY exits to kitchen. VESTA eyes the stack of funny books.)

> VESTA. You told Virgil Rivera you're selling your comic books.
> TOMMY. I need some money. I'm moving in here with Mamaw and I have to get the TV fixed.
> VESTA. Remember the day we read them together, you and I and your granddad?
> TOMMY. So?
> VESTA. Your grandfather gave them all to you in writing and all?
> TOMMY. I think so.
> VESTA. Wow. You possess an extensive and rare collection of comic books.
> TOMMY. I know.
> VESTA. I liked it where this snake woman saves the world by sucking the venom from the foot of this monster.
> TOMMY. Yeah, that was Papaw's favorite. Ramona the Revenger. She disguises herself as snakes ... she covers herself with poisonous snakes so no one will see her. Papaw bought it in 1940.
> VESTA. Whoa. Ancient times.... That's practically stone age comics.
> TOMMY. Or before.
> VESTA. Which one is your favorite?
> TOMMY. I said. Ramona, the Revenger.
> VESTA. Chill. You said that was your Papaw's.
> TOMMY. She's my favorite, too.

VESTA. OK.
TOMMY. She has tits the size of watermelons and they shoot fire. She incinerates the evil forces with her snake tongue.
VESTA. I'd like to read that one. Want to?
TOMMY. No.
VESTA. OK, so.... How much are you asking for the collection?
TOMMY. Uh, I haven't said.
VESTA. Because you haven't decided or you don't know?
TOMMY. Uh, not saying I don't know.
VESTA. Could we read one now?
TOMMY. No.
VESTA. Well, could I look at them?
TOMMY. No! Leave me alone.

(MAMAW follows POLLY to the bedrooms.)

MAMAW. If that's where you left it, that's where it is. I don't touch a thing in that room.

(TOMMY gets up to follow her.)

TOMMY. Mamaw.
MAMAW. *(Very harsh.)* I'm busy, young man.

(They are gone. TOMMY stops. He returns to Papaw's chair.)

VESTA. Would you consider a barter deal?
TOMMY. What is that?
VESTA. Where you give a person something they want for something you want.
TOMMY. I don't want nothing from nobody.

(VESTA crosses to Papaw's chair and kneels beside it.)

VESTA. I know where you are. I was like that for a long time. I'd just see everything as bad and not care about nothing. But there's good things. *(Beat.)* I'd like to sit in your lap. *(TOMMY is quiet. She does.)* You asked that slut Tandy Woo to have sex. Why didn't you ask me?

TOMMY. I don't know.
VESTA. Well, ask me.
TOMMY. I found someone.
VESTA. You did?
TOMMY. Mamaw.
VESTA. Your grandmother?
TOMMY. Yes.
VESTA. What about her?
TOMMY. She's goin' to have sex with me.
VESTA. Isn't she kinda old?
TOMMY. I don't think so.

(VESTA snuggles up to him.)

VESTA. And, you *want* to have sex with her?
TOMMY. I like her.
VESTA. Don't you like me?
TOMMY. Not a whole lot.
VESTA. You let me read your comic books.
TOMMY. You keep callin' them comic books, they're funny books. Papaw called them funny books.
VESTA. OK, funny books.
TOMMY. I let you read one of them the one time, we looked through them with Papaw. I did that.
VESTA. If you and I have sex, then you won't have to bother your grandmother. *(TOMMY is silent.)* You sign a paper makin' me your sales agent, and I'll sell 'em all and take a percentage off the top ... say 35%. I know 35% is kinda high, but as a barter situation ... I'll also have sex with you.
TOMMY. Hmmm.
VESTA. It's a good deal. Your mamaw will never have sex with you.

(TOMMY pushes VESTA away and crosses to CSL.)

TOMMY. YES, SHE WILL! GET OFF ME!

(VESTA recovers.)

VESTA. OK, but your mamaw will flip your lights off if you ask her.
TOMMY. I did ask her.
VESTA. And?
TOMMY. She said she would.
VESTA. Wow. Well. Weird. OK, then.
TOMMY. OK.
VESTA. If she changes her mind ....
TOMMY. About what?
VESTA. If she won't have sex with you ….
TOMMY. Why would she change her mind?
VESTA. Look, I have a two-year financial growth plan, so if your grandmother changes her mind ... get back to me?

(VESTA crosses to TOMMY. He has retreated against the DSL wall. She corners him.)

TOMMY. OK, I'm sorry I pushed you.
VESTA. It's OK. And Coach Norris is scared of your mother, so he won't press charges.

(A beat.)

TOMMY. If I did give you the funny books to sell for me?
VESTA. Yes?
TOMMY. We could have sex once.
VESTA. Yeah.
TOMMY. But after that I'm going to live with Mamaw.
VESTA. OK. That would be OK.
TOMMY. So don't get crazy if I don't do it more than the one time.
VESTA. No. I could live with it.

THE PARKER FAMILY CIRCUS

(MAMAW enters.)

VESTA. So, Mrs. Parker, you're going to have sex with Tommy?

TOMMY. Shut your big mouth, Vesta!

VESTA. Why? *(TOMMY flees to the bedroom. VESTA flops in Mamaw's rocker.)* He shoulda said something if he didn't want me tellin'.

MAMAW. Vesta, this is between me and Tommy ... and, well, now it's between you and me and Tommy. Don't tell Polly. Don't tell your mother, not your stepdaddy, not your real daddy, not Tommy's daddy or mother ....

VESTA. OK, OK, but are you going to do it?

MAMAW. No.

VESTA. Wow, Tommy's totally believing you will.

MAMAW. Tommy's confused.

VESTA. But, where did he get the idea?

MAMAW. Vesta. He just took a notion. Nothing has happened. Nothing is going to happen. It just looks bad. For goodness sake, don't tell anyone. They'll blame Papaw and since Papaw's dead, they'll blame me double.

VESTA. Like when my stepdaddy drug Mama across the floor by her hair in front of us kids and I called the police.

MAMAW. That's terrible, Vesta.

VESTA. They charged him with assault and child abuse. And my stepdaddy told me he was going to kick my butt to Ft. Worth and back he was so pissed at me, and now Mama is sending me off to private school.

(DON PARKER enters. A good-looking man, he has a worried but easy manner. He holds a cell phone.)

DON. Hi, Mama.

MAMAW. Lottie went over to sell your house to some woman. I asked her to do a simple thing, take Tommy home ... so now you're here, you can take him.

(MAMAW exits to the kitchen. DON makes a phone call, talks to VESTA as he dials.)

DON. Hmmm. Vesta.
VESTA. Heh, Mr. Parker.
DON. Winning anymore chess championships?
VESTA. I never won any.
DON. I thought you won a couple.
VESTA. Last year, I come close to winning some. This year, I lost.
DON. Really?
VESTA. Once, I placed third, then I got a second place, and I didn't place at all in the last one. I tanked hard.
DON. Well. Tough competition.
VESTA. I have zero support at home so I have trouble concentrating. That's what Mrs. Parker tells me.
DON. Well, guidance counselors are there to assess and advise.
VESTA. She assesses my personal life as chaos.
DON. Mine, too. Actually, hers, too.
VESTA. I know. But I'm charting a new financial future, maybe y'all should chart one, too.

(DON is on the phone.)

DON. I'm headed to pick up the fifty. How long until you close? OK, I'll be there in thirty. Don't close early—I got some family business ... I'll make good.

(DON dials again. MAMAW enters.)

MAMAW. You know, I was friendly with Vesta's granddaddy. I should have married him instead of your father.
DON. Yeah? *(MAMAW exits. DON waits for someone to answer his call.)* You look good, Vesta.
VESTA. Thanks, Mr. Parker. You do, too.

(LOTTIE enters. DON waves at her while holding his cell phone.)

LOTTIE. Hi.
VESTA. Mrs. Parker, got a cigarette?
LOTTIE. You're too young to smoke. And, you don't smoke. You sell them to young kids. A dollar a smoke. And if I catch you at it on the playground again, I'll see you get expelled.
VESTA. They'll just buy them from someone else.

(DON gets his call.)

DON. I'm picking up 50 in Plano. Have them FedEx me the 100 from Austin. I'll be back when I get back. Look. I don't question you so don't question me!
LOTTIE. Don't I hear your mother calling?
VESTA. No. Wow. So ... OK.

(VESTA exits to the kitchen.)

LOTTIE. Did I get you out of bed?
DON. Lottie ....
LOTTIE. So?
DON. What?
LOTTIE. Why were you in Plano? Did I get you out of bed? *(LOTTIE crosses to DON, sniffs.)* Break up your lunch time tryst? Do I smell the scent of "eau de Joy"? That's her favorite, how can she afford it on a production assistant's salary?

(DON crosses US behind sofa.)

DON. We're loading in a ten-truck rock 'n roller—I'm understaffed. I've got hotshot cowboys crawling around hundred-foot rafters who don't understand my rigging ....
LOTTIE. So, what are you doing driving around Plano? The arena is downtown ... there's a discrepancy in this story.
DON. I'm buying cable connectors. A lot of them.
LOTTIE. The head of production chasing connectors.
DON. We had some vandalism.

LOTTIE. Really.

(Don's cell phone rings. He answers. LOTTIE sits on the sofa.)

LOTTIE. You expect me to believe that cockamamie story? The head of production is out running around miles from the arena, shopping? You don't have gofers, like Miss What's-her-name? I think you should tell me her name ... after all, I should know her better ... she's practically part of my family.

DON. Yello. Talk to me. I'm at my mother's. No. No. The Music Hall only had 50. How many can be repaired? There's some store over toward Denton ... I think there is ... . *(Beat.)* Just hold it together until I get back! Don't answer any questions! I'm not reporting it to the police. I take full responsibility! I don't want to hear about it! *(DON slams down the phone. Sits in Papaw's chair.)* Great! Why have I been summoned?

(POLLY enters, throws herself at her father's feet.)

POLLY. Please, please, please send me to private school. Mother ... Mother ... can Tommy move in with Mamaw so I don't have to be around him?

LOTTIE. *(To her husband.)* Why are you frowning?

DON. I don't feel too good.

LOTTIE. Bad conscience? *(Beat.)* You know, between you and Papaw ....

DON. I am not my father.

(POLLY crosses between her parents.)

POLLY. I'm going to pierce every conceivable place on my body.

LOTTIE. *(To POLLY.)* If you do, you won't be subsidized by me anymore.

POLLY. Then would you listen to me?

LOTTIE. Yes. No, we cannot afford a private school and, yes,

THE PARKER FAMILY CIRCUS 39

Tommy is moving in with Mamaw because we're all moving in with Mamaw.

POLLY. You expect me to live in this mausoleum? Mother, I am so freaked out, I'm going to have a heart attack and I'm only 16. *(Yelling.)* VESTA?

LOTTIE. Kitchen.

POLLY. You know, thank you for listening to me and being honest with your cherished child that you chose to bring into the world—a human being completely dependent on your decisions.

LOTTIE. Very good, Polly.

POLLY. Any second now, I will explode!

DON. Before you do, take my keys and go fill up my car?

POLLY. *(Crossing to her father.)* Really?

LOTTIE. She doesn't have her license ....

DON. It's up to main street.

LOTTIE. This family is in enough trouble with the law already.

DON. We are?

LOTTIE. We are. And you go in front of the judge if she gets nailed.

POLLY. Mother, everyone does it ... Dad ....

DON. That's me.

POLLY. Vesta and I are wondering why the flat line promoters at the arena booked Brittany Spears. She totally sucks. No one is going to show.

DON. Four shows—totally sold out, waiting lines.

POLLY. Unbelievable. She is such a slut.

LOTTIE. Polly, there's no need for that.

DON. I could put you up with the spotlight operator if you're interested in viewing the wrong-headed masses. Tomorrow night.

POLLY. How would we get there?

DON. Your mother?

(POLLY crosses and sits next to her mother on the sofa.)

POLLY. Mom?
LOTTIE. If you gain a modicum of control and leave us alone,

we'll discuss it.

POLLY. OK, and, Dad, Vesta is putting together a deal to sell Tommy's funny books.

DON. It's not going to happen.

POLLY. Do me a favor? Don't tell her I told you? I don't want her to be mad at me.

(POLLY exits to the kitchen. Don's phone rings. He answers it.)

DON. Hello ... I'll call you back in five.
LOTTIE. She just can't get enough of you, can she.

(MAMAW enters.)

MAMAW. I never thought you were willfully destructive.
DON. Mama, what's with you?
MAMAW. If we can't tell each other important things, then the good Lord help us. And Cory asks about you and I just can't say why you don't visit ... and my preacher has always thought it peculiar that you wouldn't go see your own brother in jail....

(TOMMY yells from offstage.)

TOMMY. Mamaw! Could I talk to you, please! I'm in your bedroom!!! I'll rub your shoulders!
DON. Are your shoulders hurting?
MAMAW. No!

(MAMAW exits to the kitchen.)

DON. What's up with her?
LOTTIE. You're her son, ask her.
DON. Christ. Is there anything to eat?
LOTTIE. Doesn't what's-her-name feed you?
DON. If there hadn't been a dern what's-his-name, you wouldn't be asking if there was a what's-her-name. What do you want me to do?

LOTTIE. What?

(Don's cell phone rings. He answers.)

DON. I'll call you back in five. *(To LOTTIE.)* Is there something you want from me? Or did you just call me over here to bitch at me?
LOTTIE. Take your son to work with you.
DON. What?
LOTTIE. Because, I gave my word that we would not let him out of our sight.
DON. Christ. I've got major load-in with all kinds of problems ... I can't take him ....

(LOTTIE rises and calls to MAMAW.)

LOTTIE. MAMAW?
DON. Lottie, stop bringing her into this....
LOTTIE. She's in it ... you're in it ... and I'm in it.

(MAMAW enters.)

MAMAW. What?
LOTTIE. Tell Don to take Tommy.
MAMAW. I don't care who takes him, but somebody has got to.
LOTTIE. So. You're his father.
DON. I'm pretty well tied up. *(To LOTTIE.)* You can't?
LOTTIE. I have a job, too, dear.

(TOMMY calls out.)

TOMMY. Mamaw? I'm waiting for you!!!! In the bedroom!!!
MAMAW. It's pretty simple what I'm asking.

(MAMAW exits.)

DON. I can't take him to work with me.

LOTTIE. What? Lock him in the trunk of my car?
DON. Any other day ....
LOTTIE. So, I've tried, but I just can't.
DON. Can't what?
LOTTIE. I can't fix your son's head.
DON. Well, it's not a simple thing.
LOTTIE. It's all just going to get worse. The older he gets ....
DON. What in the Sam hill is wrong here?

(DON begins fiddling with the TV. MAMAW enters.)

MAMAW. How long are y'all going to discuss this?
LOTTIE. That's a very strange question, Mamaw?
MAMAW. I don't know what's so strange about it.
LOTTIE. We're trying to figure out what to do.
MAMAW. Leave my TV alone.
DON. Obviously, I've done something to hack you off, Mama.
MAMAW. If I want it fixed, I'll fix it.

(Don's beeper goes off. He checks it.)

TOMMY. *(Offstage.)* MAMAW, IN YOUR BEDROOM!!! PLEASE COME TALK TO ME!!!

(LOTTIE exits, talking as she goes.)

LOTTIE. If you want to be part of this conversation, young man, if you want to talk to your grandmother, you will come into .... *(A door slams, offstage.)* TOMMY!!

(MAMAW exits. DON throws up his hands in disgust.)

DON. What the hell?
LOTTIE. Just ... I don't know ... fix her TV.
DON. I don't have the tools. Thing is ancient.
LOTTIE. Use Papaw's tools.

THE PARKER FAMILY CIRCUS

DON. They don't even make the parts for it anymore.

LOTTIE. Then just put your arms around me before I disintegrate? *(DON puts his arms around his wife.)* You know. What if my boy had been a genius? They have problems, too.

DON. Tommy's all right. Maybe you could give Tommy some money and drop him off at a movie.

LOTTIE. Maybe a psychiatrist.

DON. He didn't do good with the last one.

LOTTIE. No. I'd get a psychiatrist for you.

DON. C'mon, we were working toward a moment here and then you take a swipe at my backside.

(LOTTIE breaks away from DON.)

LOTTIE. Take him to a movie. The Plano police have him under house arrest!

DON. For what?

LOTTIE. Your son pissed all over everyone in school—everyone who wasn't quick enough to get out of firing range.

DON. What?

LOTTIE. He announced he was Papaw's birddog, unzipped his fly, raised his leg and pissed all over the school grounds.

DON. People saw this?

LOTTIE. Of course. And then before I or anyone else could get to him, your son stripped off every stitch of clothing and started screaming "RAMONA SUCKS MY COCK EVERY DAY."

DON. Who's Ramona?

LOTTIE. I thought it might be your girlfriend?

DON. Lottie ....

LOTTIE. Perhaps your girlfriend has an answer for dealing with that.

DON. Good God.

LOTTIE. But she doesn't have to deal with any of your family issues, does she? She's just in it for the fun and the sex, right?

DON. If I could find Papaw's long-nosed pliers, maybe I could locate the bug up your butt. Just because you slept with some yokel.

LOTTIE. He was not some yokel, he was a very good-looking man.
DON. Fine.
LOTTIE. With a lot of money, a very big IQ and a massive—
DON . Stop it! Now, just stop it, Lottie!
LOTTIE. After Tommy pissed and stripped, he socked Jim Norris. Decked him. Out cold for five minutes. He may press charges.
DON. I played football with Sam Norris. He won't press charges. *(Don's phone rings. He checks it.)* I've got to take this ....

(DON answers his cell phone.)

LOTTIE. Oh! I JUST CAN'T GET THROUGH TO YOU! As long as we keep jumping through our hoops ... you're much more interested in your little piece on the side.
DON. Stop calling me! I can't help you! I'm coming back! *(To LOTTIE.)* When do you think I have time for anything? You writing checks left and right ....
LOTTIE. I make half the money in this household!

(DON turns off his cell phone.)

DON. And spend four times the money ... drawing up plans for a thirty-two room house with three stories, four-car garage and thirteen bathrooms. What the hell do we need all those rooms for?
LOTTIE. Let's just abandon ship.
DON. Face it, Lottie, you married an electrician. That's the real problem. I'm an electrician like my father was and I loved and admired him and wanted to grow up to be just like him. I didn't want to go to college ... I hate books and I love televisions!

(From the kitchen, sounds of pots and pans hitting the floor. LOTTIE exits to the kitchen.)

LOTTIE. Mamaw! Are you all right?

THE PARKER FAMILY CIRCUS

(DON takes the phone call. TOMMY enters from the hallway.)

TOMMY. Mamaw!
DON. What? Don't let her into the arena! No! Throw her out! I know she's a woman! *(TOMMY exits into the kitchen.)* What? Let me talk to her. I don't care if she doesn't want to— *(MAMAW enters from the kitchen and heads for the bedroom.)* What do you want from me? Get out of the arena! Now!! *(TOMMY follows MAMAW to the bedroom.)* You're lucky you're not a man! I'd beat the shit out of you!

(MAMAW enters from the bedroom and crosses to the front door. TOMMY follows her.)

TOMMY. Mamaw!
MAMAW. I CAN'T BE IN MY OWN HOUSE!
DON. Don't you hang up ... Tommy! I want to talk to you!

(LOTTIE enters from the kitchen in time to see TOMMY exiting out the front door.)

LOTTIE. Stop right there! Do not step outside that door! *(She looks out the door.)* MAMAW! *(Straight at TOMMY.)* Don't you move! Stay here! *(Calling.)* MAMAW!

(LOTTIE exits to the yard.)

DON. Listen, you little sack of shit. You tell Mr. Muckity Muck about this and I'll tell him every time I've covered your ass—
TOMMY. Mamaw!
DON. I know the trucks are coming! I'll cut you up and use you for fish bait ....
TOMMY. ... use you for fish bait ....
DON. I'll rip off your head and puke down your throat ....
TOMMY. ... puke down your throat ....
DON. Just smile at them and say, "Mr. Parker has it under control."
TOMMY. Mamaw ....

(Blackout.)

END OF ACT ONE

ACT II

(The action replays the end of Act I. DON speaks on the phone and TOMMY watches out the front door)

DON. I'll rip off your head and puke down your throat ....
TOMMY. ... puke down your throat ....
DON. Just smile at them and say, "Mr. Parker has it under control."

(DON hangs up.)

TOMMY. Mamaw ... Daddy, why is Mamaw standing in the front yard?
DON. I think she had a sort of kitchen catastrophe.
TOMMY. Did she hear me calling her?
DON. I believe she did.

(DON crosses to HIS son. Places a hand on his shoulder.)

TOMMY. Is she mad at me?
DON. No.

(TOMMY crosses to the television.)

TOMMY. Can you fix Papaw's TV?
DON. Not right now. Tommy, I need to talk to you. Son ... what's going on with you?

(TOMMY crosses to Papaw's chair. He is very sad. DON sits on the

window seat.)

TOMMY. This morning, I saw this man that looked a lot like Papaw but it wasn't him.

DON. No.

TOMMY. His hat was the same. Papaw had a black hat he wore a lot. Where's that hat?

DON. I don't know.

TOMMY. And he wore baseball caps sometimes. One was the Cowboys because they used to win a lot of games.

DON. Yeah, they used to.

TOMMY. I don't care about that team now.

DON. No?

TOMMY. It was only fun because Papaw and me watched the games together. And we'd read the funny books.

DON. I know.

TOMMY. But nobody reads them anymore with me like he did.

DON. We used to read together.

TOMMY. But you always wanted me to say the right words and I couldn't do that a lot. Papaw didn't care. He did it just so we could be together. *(MAMAW enters. LOTTIE follows her cautiously. The women exit to the kitchen.)* What's going to happen to me?

DON. You got in some trouble today?

TOMMY. I remembered today, Papaw brought me Birddog home in his lunch box. And Birddog died right after Papaw died.

DON. Birddog was real old.

TOMMY. But, he didn't die because he was old. Why he died was because Birddog got to looking for Papaw and couldn't find him and he just got so sad.

DON. Yeah. We're all sad, Tommy. But we can't just start doing crazy things.

TOMMY. I'm selling my funny books. Vesta's going to sell 'em for me.

DON. I can't let you do that, Tommy.

TOMMY. Why?

DON. Some of them are mine but some are Uncle Cory's and

Papaw gave 'em to you but he didn't give 'em to you to sell. He gave them to you to protect so you could hand them down.

TOMMY. Hand them down to who?

DON. To your kids.

TOMMY. I don't think they'll let me have kids when I'm in jail.

DON. You're not going to jail.

TOMMY. What's going to happen to me?

DON. Right now, I think you're fixing to come with me.

TOMMY. No. I'm staying here and I'm selling my funny books.

DON. Son. Those funny books are special.

TOMMY. Not so much. You can watch 'em on TV or some people watch 'em on the computers and such. They don't even show 'em at the movies anymore unless it's for little bitty kids.

DON. They're worth a lot of money.

TOMMY. I need money. I'm coming to live with Mamaw. I'm not going back to school, they're just letting me graduate on account of Mother.

DON. Who told you that?

TOMMY. The coach. He called me an idiot. Papaw told me, the next time that man calls you an idiot, draw back and knock his block off.

DON. Papaw didn't mean that. He was kidding.

TOMMY. Nuh unh. Papaw never would kid me. I hit him real hard. My hand hurts. It's getting all swollen up. You can't make me go back to school.

DON. Let me see it. *(TOMMY winces as DON examines his hand.)* It's OK. What would you do instead of going back to school?

TOMMY. Work.

DON. At what?

TOMMY. With you?

DON. They don't have any jobs where I work.

TOMMY. Well. I could just hang around with you.

DON. You'd get in the way.

TOMMY. I'd work in Papaw's shop. Put a sign outside saying Tommy's Shop.

DON. And then?

TOMMY. Well, fix things. I could learn how to fix television sets. Like you and Papaw did.

DON. Televisions were made a lot different back then.

TOMMY. Well, I'd just fix old television sets.

DON. I don't think there's any old ones left. They're in museums.

TOMMY. Well. I'll just take care of Mamaw so she don't die. When y'all move she won't have no one. She's very old. And she's like me, nobody wants her.

DON. Now, that's not right.

TOMMY. I'd protect her.

DON. Sounds to me like she might need protection from you.

TOMMY. Why?

DON. Your mother says you don't know where to find the pisser.

TOMMY. I know where it is.

DON. Your mother works hard at that school.

TOMMY. All the kids at school hate her. They call her the head shrinker.

DON. Your mother's frustrated. You know what frustrated means?

TOMMY. No. I don't know what anything means. I'm dumb.

DON. Tommy ....

TOMMY. I am. I'm not like Polly. She can do anything. I'm four years older than she is and she's a junior and I'm a senior. What's going to happen to me? They'll send me to jail like Uncle Cory.

DON. Uncle Cory. Now, Polly, she's more likely to end up like him.

TOMMY. She don't do nothing wrong.

DON. Neither did Cory. Daddy always said Cory could pull a TV apart and put it back together in the same time it took me to scratch my butt. You and me, we're more methodical.

TOMMY. I don't know what that means.

DON. We go at things a little slower but we get them done. You know, I had my trouble when I was your age.

TOMMY. No, Dad. You never did have trouble like me. It's OK, Daddy. You're just trying to make me feel better.

DON. Yes, I guess I am.
TOMMY. I thought you were thinking Mamaw was scared of me because I asked her to have sex with me.
DON. What?
TOMMY. Maybe Mamaw and me could have a baby and the baby could get the funny books when I die.

(DON loses it. Explodes.)

DON. I oughta beat the crap out of you, boy.

(DON stands, furious. POLLY enters, euphoric. Jumps and embraces her father. VESTA follows.)

POLLY. Dad! Dad! I, like, saw everyone I know at the I-Hop and they all said it was, like, a rip-off about student council. And Mother agrees that they have to prove incompetency, so Vesta's going to start a petition and put a spin on the whole thing ....
DON. Polly, get out of here.
TOMMY. And, Daddy, Vesta said she'd have sex with me, too.
VESTA. Kidding!

(VESTA exits to the kitchen.)

DON. Tommy, stop. Stop talking.
POLLY. Dad, Vesta's very together that way.
TOMMY. If I let Vesta sell Papaw's funny books, she's gonna have sex with me one time.
DON. This has got to stop!
POLLY. Have you lost it?
DON. Vesta's out of this house!
POLLY. Dad! Vesta sees a money-making venture and she goes for it, you can't blame her.
DON. Define prostitution.
POLLY. Sexual services for pay, that's physical ... and moral prostitution is like ....

DON. I've stumbled into this black hole!
POLLY. Dad, Vesta and I believe prostitution should be legalized.
DON. I should tape this bull and play it back to you in forty years.
POLLY. It's not bull, Dad. Oh, I forgot to tell you, Mamaw is like planning to go to Nicaragua. Don't tell her I told you, OK?
DON. What?

(POLLY crosses to DON, hugs him.)

POLLY. Stay firm, Dad.

(She exits to the kitchen. LOTTIE enters with a serving of peach cobbler.)

LOTTIE. Peach cobbler—fabulous. Want some, Tommy?

(TOMMY rises, calls to the kitchen.)

TOMMY. Mamaw, I going back to the bedroom. I'm waiting for you!!!

(He exits to the bedroom. DON sits on the window seat.)

LOTTIE. Every time I come into the room, you get up and stomp out. It won't work much longer, Tommy. Don? Cobbler?

(DON's cell phone rings.)

DON. No. I've got heartburn.
LOTTIE. You're missing a great peach cobbler—divine.

(DON turns off his cell phone.)

DON. Lottie, I'm going to lose my job.

THE PARKER FAMILY CIRCUS 53

(LOTTIE crosses to sofa. Sits.)

LOTTIE. Great. We'll both lose our jobs, we'll be the only welfare recipients who own a thirty-six room house with a mortgage.
DON. I've got to find 1500 male connectors.
LOTTIE. You keep going on about connectors.
DON. This woman on the electrics crew went psycho and castrated all the cables. I have 1500 cables with a female connector and no male connector.
LOTTIE. Why would she do such a thing?
DON. Because she's crazy. Everyone is crazy.
LOTTIE. Was it what's-her-name?
DON. Yes.
LOTTIE. She vandalized your shop?
DON. Yes.
LOTTIE. Well, we'll be seeing more of you at home.

(DON crosses to sofa. Sits with LOTTIE.)

DON. Lottie, I told her it was over. I told her I'd made a mistake. I didn't want to lose my family. She pitched a wall-eyed fit.
LOTTIE. I shouldn't be your wife. I shouldn't be Tommy's mother.
DON. I should just blow all our brains out.
LOTTIE. Why bother. We'll both be dead from stress in ten years.

(POLLY and VESTA enter. POLLY crosses to CS and reads from notebook paper. VESTA sits in Mamaw's rocker.)

POLLY. Mom, listen to this ....
LOTTIE. Polly, not now.
POLLY. It will just take a second. *(Reading.)* As the faculty advisor, Mrs. Bristow, was not present at the April 15th meeting of the student council, the meeting was not officially supervised. Whereas, the motion made by Connie Mercedes and seconded by Mike Potts to

relieve Polly Pearl Parker from her post as junior class representative was voted on and passed without faculty supervision, it is null and void ....

LOTTIE. Polly ....

POLLY. Vesta thinks we should threaten them ... something like, any subsequent harassment of Ms. Parker will result in a lawsuit against the student council and the Greater Plano School District.

VESTA. Yes!

LOTTIE. Can we discuss this later?

POLLY. What do you think? I could be totally overreacting and these cheese balls could whip around and say, "Heh, can't you take a joke?"

LOTTIE. Polly, would you just, I don't know, just ....

POLLY. Mom, I want to take this over to school now while they're still there.

LOTTIE. I'll look at it later. Go home.

VESTA. Uh, that woman is coming back ....

LOTTIE. Lord, I forgot about her. Then, go to Vesta's.

VESTA. I'm locked out of my house until 8:30.

POLLY. Can we drive Dad's van back to the I-Hop?

LOTTIE. No.

POLLY. Why?

LOTTIE. Why does a simple request become a debate? Just go sit on the porch until we decide what to do about Tommy.

(POLLY sits in Papaw's chair.)

POLLY. Drop him in a vat of boiling oil.

LOTTIE. You know, Polly, you're a mono-maniac. You don't possess an ounce of sympathy.

POLLY. That is so unfair.

LOTTIE. I'm not feeling fair.

POLLY. Every time Tommy screws up, I suffer for it. It always comes back to *me*.

LOTTIE. There's suffering and there's slight discomfort.

POLLY. OK, but if I am a mono-maniac, it's your fault because I have to throw myself in front of a moving bus to get any attention whatsoever. Let's blow this pop stand.

(POLLY and VESTA exit to the porch. LOTTIE gazes at DON.)

LOTTIE. I was so hoping that I was just paranoid, and nothing was going on with you. What a fool ... smiling through ....

(MAMAW enters. LOTTIE crosses USR.)

MAMAW. I'm fixing to go visit Cory so get your son and go home.
LOTTIE. Mamaw, we're going to see Cory on Sunday.
MAMAW. I'm going tonight.
LOTTIE. Does the prison allow visitors at night?
MAMAW. I'm lonely to see my poor baby. Little Cory never gets to bite into a fresh baked pie. He can't just waltz into my kitchen and slice himself a piece of pie, uninvited.
LOTTIE. I thought those pies were for the church auction.
MAMAW. I can't auction a pie with a big hole in it.
LOTTIE. Don, just give her thirty dollars.
DON. Thirty dollars for a pie ....
LOTTIE. It's for charity.

(DON fumbles for money. Gives it to MAMAW.)

MAMAW. Thank you. I want to leave here as soon as I can.
DON. Mama, are you all right?
MAMAW. Of course I'm all right. Why wouldn't I be all right?
LOTTIE. She said she wasn't feeling well.
MAMAW. I'm feeling fine. *(To DON.)* Why are you looking at me like that?
DON. We've got a situation here and I'm wondering what to do about it.
MAMAW. You can do what I've asked you to, take your son home.

DON. I'm a little confused, Mama.
MAMAW. There's nothing to be confused about. I'm fixing to go visit Cory.
LOTTIE. Mamaw, they won't allow you on the prison grounds.
MAMAW. I'm friendly with those people that work there.
LOTTIE. Because we do exactly what they tell us to do. You have no special permission, no birthday, no death ....
MAMAW. Let me worry about that.
LOTTIE. Tomorrow's Saturday. We'll go tomorrow.
MAMAW. Don't want to go tomorrow. I'm going as soon as you leave and I lock up my house.
DON. What happened between you and Tommy, Mama?
MAMAW. Nothing happened.
DON. Did Tommy scare you?
LOTTIE. Is that it?
MAMAW. Nobody scared me. Now quit asking me questions.
LOTTIE. Mamaw, don't be so sharp with us.
MAMAW. I have never been "sharp" in my life.

(MAMAW picks up LOTTIE's dirty pie plate and exits to kitchen.)

LOTTIE. Mamaw, I was going to do that.… *(Clanking in the kitchen.)* Is it Cory ....
DON. Lottie, this is touchy ....
LOTTIE. What?

(MAMAW enters.)

DON. Mama ....
MAMAW. And I can't believe you would tell Polly that you were scared I'd die without Papaw.
DON. Well, you've been quiet.
MAMAW. I haven't seen you, how would you know if I've been quiet?
DON. Lottie? Didn't you say ....
LOTTIE. … don't do that!

THE PARKER FAMILY CIRCUS

MAMAW. And you told Polly my dear little mother died from loneliness. She died from high blood pressure because she forgot to take her medicine.

DON. I just remembered her being kinda depressed.

MAMAW. She was a serious woman, she was not depressed. She was never lonely. I was with her.

DON. Well then, I'm sorry. I was wrong.

(POLLY and VESTA enter from the porch. They cross USR.)

POLLY. You do not see us. We are invisible ... we are not walking through this room .... *(They exit to the hall.)* Tommy! What are you doing?

(Scuffling. Running feet. A door slam.)

MAMAW. And I don't want these kids spending time over here. I won't be here.

DON. Polly tells me you're planning some kind of trip.

MAMAW. The preacher is taking a group to rebuild Nicaragua.

(MAMAW puts on her sweater, gathers her purse, shuts windows, prepares to leave the house.)

DON. You haven't stepped foot out of Texas that I remember.

MAMAW. And the preacher asked me if I wanted to sign up. And I did.

DON. Well, what part of Nicaragua would you rebuild?

MAMAW. Whatever they need rebuilt.

DON. Mama. Give me a chance here.

MAMAW. I have plans of my own, they may not coincide with your family's plans.

DON. All right. You can go if you want to ....

LOTTIE. Are you out of your mind? Nicaragua is unsafe.

MAMAW. Halloween night, there was a little kid right down the block, got robbed of all his candy by bigger kids with baseball bats.

LOTTIE. Those kids were from South Dallas.

MAMAW. Just as much can happen here in Plano, Texas, as can happen in the middle of little Nicaragua. And I'm a good handyman. I repaired this house for sixty years. I can do plumbing and electricity.

DON. Maybe you ought to come work for me at the arena.

MAMAW. Don't get sarcastic with me.

DON. Mama, just level with me here.

(MAMAW crosses to DON on the sofa.)

MAMAW. After Papaw's first heart attack, he prepared for "the big one" as he called it—he took out an expensive insurance policy.

DON. I picked it out.

MAMAW. I hear you picked out Cory's jail cell, too.

DON. What?

MAMAW. I can afford to do purt near anything I want. We raised two kids off his paycheck from Bell Helicopter of $440 a month and what he got for repairing TVs.

DON. He worked hard, Mama ....

MAMAW. We both worked hard. And there was a lot we did without.

LOTTIE. Meaning?

MAMAW. Meaning, I don't see you going without. Running here and running there. Buying this and that ... you have so much you don't even know what you have ... putting on shows and selling houses, that's the easy part ... raising children, that's the hard part, so you just stepped back and let us do that.

LOTTIE. I didn't step back. Papaw stepped in. Papaw wanted Tommy to live with you. Hell, he wanted us all to live with you. I refused, so he upped me one better, he made a down payment on a house right across the street ....

DON. We were broke as I remember.

LOTTIE. We're still broke. Papaw sucked us in ... handed you the deed to a house instead of a college education. Ruined Cory.

DON. The man's dead, Lottie. And Cory ruined Cory.

MAMAW. Don't talk that way about my boy!

(DON rises, crosses US of sofa.)

DON. Mama, let's talk about you and Tommy.
MAMAW. I'll talk about what I want to talk about. Did you turn your brother over to the police?
DON. Where the hell did that come from?
MAMAW. What does it matter?
DON. I want to know who told you.
MAMAW. Tommy.
DON. Well, who told him?
MAMAW. Papaw.
DON. Tommy can't remember which way is up but he can remember anything Daddy ever said.
MAMAW. You turned my Cory over to the police?
DON. Yes, by God!
MAMAW. Well, why would you do a thing like that?
DON. Because my brother, your precious Cory, came home to borrow twenty thousand dollars from Daddy. And my father was about to mortgage your house so Cory could start a new life in another country, so I turned Cory over to the law. I knew where he was hiding and I told them. I'm sorry if you're disappointed in me.

(MAMAW sits on the sofa.)

MAMAW. He told me that he borrowed those people's money ....
DON. He *stole* a lot of people's money.
MAMAW. But he's going to make good on it when he gets out of jail.
DON. Mama. If that's what you want to believe, that's fine by me.
MAMAW. Lottie, is this true?
LOTTIE. Yes.
MAMAW. And Daddy knew about it?
DON. Mama, you were so torn up ....
MAMAW. He was trying to protect me, because he loved me more'n anything in the world.

DON. Can't argue with that.

MAMAW. Cory used to take money out of my pocketbook when he was little. I never could get him to see that it was wrong. You never took a nickel.

DON. No.

MAMAW. I'll take responsibility for Cory. But I can't take responsibility for Tommy.

(POLLY and VESTA enter.)

POLLY. OK, we're coming back through with two questions and one observation.

LOTTIE. What?

POLLY. Question number one—if we get to go see Brittany Spears ... which I am hoping that we'll get to do fully knowing we might not ... but, if we're still going to get to do that ... can we stop at Neiman's and exchange the top you bought me for my birthday ... the one that's too small ....

LOTTIE. We'll try.

POLLY. And question number two, can we please have some pie?

MAMAW. Your mother bought the peach cobbler.

POLLY. Thanks. And, the observation ... Tommy is sitting in the hallway listening to every word you say.

LOTTIE. Tommy?

POLLY. We're history.

(The girls exit to the kitchen.)

LOTTIE. Tommy?

(She exits to the hall. Door slam. DON sits on sofa with MAMAW.)

DON. So. How long would you be staying in Nicaragua? Six weeks, a year....

MAMAW. I don't have to tell you.

THE PARKER FAMILY CIRCUS

DON. No, I guess you don't.
MAMAW. I've got family all over this world that I haven't met that I've been sponsoring through the church for years, and those people in Nicaragua, they've lost everything in this last flood.

(LOTTIE enters. Sits in Papaw's chair.)

DON. Send them a check.
MAMAW. Daddy got to see Europe in the Army, but the only time I traveled was when we went to see my sister in Brownsville but he got so homesick....
LOTTIE. You sacrificed a lot.
MAMAW. I never sacrificed a thing. I didn't like going off and leaving him. So if he didn't go, I didn't want to go.
LOTTIE. Well, OK.
DON. Now, c'mon, Mama, you're too old to be in the dern Peace Corps.
MAMAW. The preacher says I'd be an asset.
DON. That damn preacher will get everyone killed.
MAMAW. ... and these kids ... I don't know where these kids get these ideas....
DON. Mama, this situation is awkward as hell but we're going to have to talk about it.
LOTTIE. Mamaw. Don has problems at work. I've got this meeting. I don't want to go into the details, but they'll do everything they can to keep Tommy out of school this time. Criminal charges....

(TOMMY calls from the hallway.)

TOMMY. I'm not going back to that school. You can just forget it!
LOTTIE. Tommy!

(Footsteps and a door slam. POLLY and VESTA enter and cross USC, carrying pie.)

POLLY. I wish she had bought the coconut ... this is like gooey.

VESTA. I don't know. I kind of like it.

(They exit to the porch.)

MAMAW. Tommy is like Morris Puckett.
DON. Who is Morris Puckett?
MAMAW. He was my first cousin. He died at thirty. Climbed in an old ice box and pulled the door shut, couldn't get out.
DON. I remember that.
MAMAW. Morris started off a little weak-minded but then later on he had a fall off a horse ... well, actually it wasn't a fall, he was riding hard down a dirt road and there was a gate where the horse turned and Morris didn't—he just kept going straight—and hit a fence post. Bam! Now, Morris was slow to begin with but after hitting that post head-on, he was real slow.
LOTTIE. Mamaw ....
MAMAW. Now, he was my first cousin on Daddy's side and even before this accident with the horse, I remember his mother telling my mother that she was going to stop having kids because there was some slowness on that side of the family ... that whole line. Well. Could be that slowness has worked its way down to Tommy. It never occurred to me before this, but I think there's a connection. I don't know. Maybe I shouldn't have had children.
LOTTIE. Don and I dropped LSD.
DON. Lottie ....
LOTTIE. We did. We climbed over the fence at the Dallas Rock Festival—at the speedway—the summer of '69.
DON. Lottie ....
LOTTIE. We waited to start a family until I got my master's and then until we paid off my student loan, and then until we paid off the mortgage, but I was really waiting because I was scared the acid had thrown my teratogens out of whack.
DON. Lottie, I think that was some kind of scare tactic.
LOTTIE. You always say that.
DON. Because it's true.
LOTTIE. You're probably right. Could be pollution, bad Chinese

food. Mamaw. I know Tommy's a handful without Papaw here but we'll talk to him.

MAMAW. You can't even get him to come out of my bedroom.

LOTTIE. We're in so deep with building the new house and mother in a nursing home ... I was even thinking, what if Tommy came to live with you after school is over, until we decide what to do.

MAMAW. No.

LOTTIE. No?

DON. No.

LOTTIE. Why?

DON. Not a good idea. Let's go.

LOTTIE. Where are we going?

DON. Just ... do what I'm asking.

LOTTIE. Tommy needs you more than ever. Why can't he stay here?

DON. Because it's her house and she said she wanted him out.

(VESTA sticks her head in the house.)

VESTA. I know why.

MAMAW. Vesta, I hate being rude but I'll ask you to keep your little mouth shut and out of my business. *(VESTA closes the porch door.)* I wouldn't listen to much that girl says. I believe she's a bit of a liar.

DON. She's ... Well ... could be. *(DON exits to bedroom. Calling.)* Tommy!

LOTTIE. I never thought Vesta a liar. Actually, she is painfully truthful.

MAMAW. Call me a liar, why don't you?

LOTTIE. I didn't call you a liar.

MAMAW. Papaw and I were just unpaid babysitters. From the time Tommy had trouble learning his colors, I told him you all shoulda done something. But Papaw would say, "Leave that child alone, he's not going to be a house painter."

DON. *(Offstage.)* Tommy!

MAMAW. Then he had trouble with his numbers—"He's not

going to be an accountant." Then with his reading, "He don't have the look of a lawyer." And I took a back seat but it seemed to me ....

LOTTIE. What?

MAMAW. Well, there's been a lack of interest on your part.

LOTTIE. Lack of interest? I have tried everything. Everything.

MAMAW. And all this unsettled-ness....

LOTTIE. Unsettled-ness?

MAMAW. The good Lord has given us a set of tools to work with.

LOTTIE. That's Papaw talking.

MAMAW. I have a mind of my own, Lottie Parker. I don't parrot everything Papaw said. Did you ever think that Papaw was repeating what I said?

DON. *(Offstage.)* TOMMY!

MAMAW. Papaw repeated things I said many times a day. When he came back from the Korea all crazy with ringing sounds in his ears, I had to talk to people for him for the next year practically. *(DON enters.)* He could not form a sentence. He dern near froze to death over in Korea.

LOTTIE. Don? Help me?

DON. Mama, what if I left the house. I'll go back outside. Will you feel better talking to a woman? Talk to Lottie, she's a woman.

LOTTIE. Talk to me about what?

DON. Ask her. She won't tell me. And if she won't tell you, I'm stumped. I'm paralyzed from the neck up. I'll just stand here until I haven't got a job anymore.

MAMAW. I've told you! Take your son home!

(TOMMY enters.)

    TOMMY. Please let me talk to Mamaw!
    DON. GET IN HERE! NOW!
    TOMMY. NO!

(TOMMY exits.)

    LOTTIE. Don't yell at him like that.

DON. Stay out of this, Lottie!

LOTTIE. *(Incredulous.)* Stay out of this?

DON. You told me to take him so get off my back!

LOTTIE. Don't talk to me like that in front of your mother. What's gotten into you?

DON. *(Calling.)* Tommy! LET'S GO!

TOMMY. NO!!!

(DON exits after TOMMY. A door slam.)

MAMAW. You let Tommy become an old man's pet monkey. Tommy never did nothing but what he didn't ask Papaw what he thought about it.

LOTTIE. He wanted the kids here. He wanted an audience.

MAMAW. You've got a kid that can't make it out of the nest and likely as not, never will—so you better get used to making him feel safe or he'll turn mean and kill every last one of us in our sleep.

LOTTIE. Oh, Mamaw, no.

DON. *(Offstage.)* Tommy! You open that door right now! You hear me?

MAMAW. I pray to God Almighty that that's not where it's going. I feel for you, Lottie. Resentment is a powerful curse.

LOTTIE. My butt is black and blue from you kicking it. *(DON enters.)* You talk to me like I'm this insensitive, shallow mother and that's not right, Don. I'm trying to fill my life with some movement ... all right, maybe it's in the wrong direction or in too many directions but at least I'm trying. And I want to quit. I've wanted to quit for a long time.

MAMAW. You two better *quit* your fooling around.

TOMMY. *(Offstage.)* MAMAW, PLEASE!!!

(MAMAW crosses to kitchen.)

MAMAW. I can't wait until I get shut of the bunch of you.

DON. This is about Tommy getting out of line with you.

MAMAW. Don't say another word.

DON. Mama, just tell her.
MAMAW. I don't know what you're talking about.
LOTTIE. What?

(MAMAW exits to the kitchen. DON stops her.)

DON. You'd rather go off to Nicaragua than trust us to understand? All right. Go on down to the prison and cry on Cory's shoulder. Do you think he's going to help you? Cory is a selfish little shit who never gave a damn about anybody, never has and never will.… *(MAMAW turns and slaps her son.)* Mama!
MAMAW. Leave me alone!

(Crosses DSR to the bedroom. TOMMY enters, frantic.)

TOMMY. Leave her alone! Stop yelling at her!
DON. Let's go!
TOMMY. NO!

(MAMAW crosses to the porch.)

LOTTIE. Tommy!
TOMMY. Mamaw, please talk to me! PLEASE!!! Don't tell her about us! She'll ruin everything!
LOTTIE. Tell me what?
DON. Tommy asked my mother to have sex with him.

(MAMAW turns on her son.)

MAMAW. Hush up! Hush your mouth!

(TOMMY exits to the bedroom.)

LOTTIE. TOMMY, COME BACK HERE!!!
MAMAW. DON'T CALL HIM BACK IN HERE! LOTTIE, PLEASE!!!

(LOTTIE stops DSR.)

LOTTIE. I'm so sorry.
DON. It's like you said, Mama, if we can't talk to one another then God help us. Just talk to us, Mama.

(MAMAW crosses to Papaw's chair.)

MAMAW. I've petted on him since he was a baby. Such a pretty baby, so quiet and his little smile lit up the world. When he was small, he'd let me rock him for hours. And he and Papaw, we had such a good time. Why, I'd give Papaw a haircut and then I'd give Tommy one. Then we lost Papaw. Tommy never left my side at Papaw's funeral. And all the flowers died, the condolence cards stopped coming and the living went back to living, and a blanket of grief laid so heavy on my heart I thought I'd die. Tommy found me sitting and crying so hard I couldn't stop and my boy held me and rocked me until I got quieted down. There's been times when I felt his hands wander but I thought it was my imagination. Then, he started babbling all this nonsense today and I was scared to tell you—I was scared you'd blame me ... or not be able to forgive him. And maybe I did bring it on. I was lonely for Papaw. We always touched, Papaw had a wonderful touch and it's a sad thing never to touch or be touched.
LOTTIE. Oh, my Lord my Lord ... Mamaw. He doesn't mean it.
MAMAW. Lottie. I don't feel safe with him.
LOTTIE. Mamaw. He doesn't understand what he's saying. It's all the kids at school talk—sex ... but it's harmless....
MAMAW. Lottie, as Papaw used to say, "It's every man for himself."

(LOTTIE crosses to sofa. Sits. DON joins her.)

LOTTIE. Running, running away and suddenly silence ... nothing more to say, nowhere to go ... nothing to do ...here you are. Here it is. Bam!

(She giggles.)

DON. What?

LOTTIE. Morris Puckett ... and the horse.... Reminds me. Red Rover, Red Rover—let Tommy come over!

DON. I don't remember.

LOTTIE. You blocked it out. Tommy had to get nine stitches. You about fainted watching the doctor sew up this huge gash.

DON. Oh, yeah, I got light-headed.

LOTTIE. The first grade, the kids were playing Red Rover, Red Rover. And they called Tommy. He got so excited, he put his little head down and ran into the line so hard he broke through and ran straight into the school wall. I was so worried 'cause even with blood dripping down his head and both his eyes turning black, my boy just grinned.

(DON laughs with LOTTIE.)

DON. Blood gets me every time. I almost fainted when Coon Watkins cut off his little finger with the circular saw.

LOTTIE. The doctor was sewing his scalp up and Tommy said, "They called me over, Mama, they called Red Rover, Red Rover, let Tommy come over."

MAMAW. You think that's funny, Lottie?

LOTTIE. Yes.

MAMAW. And you think that's appropriate?

LOTTIE. No. It's just I looked at that little face and I knew public school wasn't the right place for him, and Don and I talked about sending him to a special school but Papaw heard about it ... I don't know, did you tell him?

DON. I think it was Cory. I think I told Cory and Cory told Dad.

LOTTIE. And Papaw looked at me like I had sprouted horns. "It was just a little bump on the head, Lottie, could have happened to anyone. It's good for the boy." And you agreed with him.

DON. Did I?

LOTTIE. Yes, you did. You and Cory and Papaw. The three of

you ganged up on me like you had tremendous insight into the rites of manhood. Papaw brushed me aside because I was just some secondary education major. I told you Tommy's I.Q. He registered 70 and that was after hours of drilling on I.Q. tests. And Cory said, "Hell, Lottie, I can't even read and I graduated high school."

DON. I don't remember that.

LOTTIE. What are you saying, that I'm making this up?

DON. I didn't say you were making it up, I said I didn't remember it.

MAMAW. You two are going to sit here and giggle and squabble and not do a thing. You haven't done anything for twenty years. You love him but you can't help him.

LOTTIE. Let me clarify some things here. Tommy has to be supervised. Does everyone understand that? So. What do you want me to do? Drug him senseless? There's side effects to lithium and zyprexa and atavan ... and he'll be a zombie. People die from lithium poisoning. Is that what you want? You want me to send him to a special school? The ones that are worth anything are very expensive and even if we find one that will take him ... it requires applications and planning and we don't have the money. Would you like for me to follow my principal's advice and commit him to Denton State School where he'll get raped and bullied....

MAMAW. It's your problem.

LOTTIE. Yes. I guess it is. So. What next?

MAMAW. Do you want to tell Tommy or do you want me to tell him?

LOTTIE. Exactly what are we telling him?

MAMAW. That he can't come here anymore.

(MAMAW exits to the kitchen. LOTTIE rises and moves to Papaw's chair. Calls on her cell phone.)

LOTTIE. *(Dialing.)* I think I just got your indigestion. *(On the phone.)* Put up a sign. SWIP meeting canceled. Yes. Put it up. *(Redials.)* Pure dread. *(On the phone.)* Honey, Lottie Parker. Don't come back over tonight. I'll have to show it to you some other time.

I'm sorry. I know. *(The woman hangs up.)* Right.

DON. What am I supposed to do, drag him out?

LOTTIE. God. She's right. We can't even get him out of her bedroom.

DON. Should I break down the door?

LOTTIE. I guess you'll have to. I feel like I just swallowed an elephant. Tommy doesn't do well with sudden changes.

DON. If we can get to next week, I can shuffle the work load....

LOTTIE. Well, tomorrow's Saturday. I can cancel that.

DON. *(Amused.)* You can cancel Saturday?

LOTTIE. I think maybe I can.

DON. You're amazing.

LOTTIE. No, I better not. We're going to need Saturday to prepare for Monday.

DON. Are you going to cancel me?

LOTTIE. Don, if I concentrate on you, I have to concentrate on your son and then I have to acknowledge this deep, deep sadness and I know it's wrong—I shouldn't be sad. It's just that Tommy's smart enough to know to be scared. Everyone is passing him by.

DON. He'll be all right. Why did you sleep with that guy?

LOTTIE. I don't know. He didn't know me, he didn't know who I am, he didn't know who I was, he didn't know I had a family. Why did you sleep with that girl?

DON. To get even.

LOTTIE. Was she young?

DON. Yeah.

LOTTIE. The young stuff is costly.

DON. Oh, yeah. I'm sorry.

LOTTIE. Well, me too.

DON. You know, believe it or not, out of all the people in this world, you're the only person who knows who I am ... don't give up.

(A beat. On the porch, POLLY and VESTA yell at someone in the distance.)

POLLY. Heh! Heh, you!!! HEH!!!!

THE PARKER FAMILY CIRCUS

VESTA. HEH!
LOTTIE. *(To the porch.)* Who are you yelling at?
POLLY. Some boy! He looks like Brad Pitt!!!
LOTTIE. Well, stop it! Standing out on the porch yelling like a lunatic.

(The girls enter, giggling.)

POLLY. He saw you!
VESTA. He saw YOU!
POLLY. He waved!!!
LOTTIE. One minute you're political activists, then entrepreneurs, now you're monkeys.

(The girls exit to the porch.)

POLLY. *(Outside.)* WHAT'S YOUR NAME???
DON. I never heard Mama raise her voice before.
LOTTIE. *(Watching the girls.)* Unbelievable.

(MAMAW enters, composed.)

MAMAW. You two haven't accomplished much, have you? I thought you were in such a hurry to get back to work. Papaw used to say that he was the ring master and I said I cleaned up after the animal acts. Well, not anymore. *(She yells out to the porch.)* POLLY, VESTA ....

(POLLY enters.)

POLLY. We're talking to the cutest boy!
MAMAW. Now, listen here, young lady, I want you in here. You've got to start pulling your weight in this family.
POLLY. Mamaw ....
LOTTIE. Polly, just come in and sit down. Don, will you do something with her?

DON. Lighten up, Lottie, at least she's not depressed.
POLLY. Is someone depressed?
MAMAW. Vesta, I want you in here, too. You're so interested in what's going on in this family.
VESTA. Chill....

(VESTA sits in Mamaw's rocker. POLLY sits on the floor beside her. DON sits in Papaw's chair. LOTTIE sits on the window seat.)

MAMAW. Now. We're going to do something different. We're going to *all* be in the same room at the same time. *(LOTTIE's cell phone rings.)* And I want everything that beeps turned off. *(MAMAW exits for the bedroom.)* TOMMY! GET IN HERE!

(LOTTIE answers her cell phone.)

LOTTIE. Lottie Parker. Yes. Yes. Could you give me one second? *(To DON.)* The police ... they're checking in ... what do I tell them?
DON. Tell them we'll be at the arena. They can watch us unload ten semis with two million teenagers screaming, "Brittany."
LOTTIE. Hello ... Tommy Parker will be with his parents. Yes. You can reach me at this number. Yes, I understand. *(She disconnects.)* That was ominous.
POLLY. Is Tommy going to be arrested?
LOTTIE. No. Vesta, Tommy's comic books are not for sale. And, a mercenary is not a nice person.
VESTA. I'm a survivalist, Mrs. Parker, not a mercenary.
POLLY. I don't get it. What's going to happen?
LOTTIE. It'll be OK.
VESTA. You simplify everything, Mrs. Parker.
LOTTIE. I do?
VESTA. You're paid to do that at school so I guess you get in a habit of it. Probably, like selling real estate helps.
LOTTIE. You think?
VESTA. Yeah, because when something's too difficult to fathom,

THE PARKER FAMILY CIRCUS

you can do something practical like sell a house.
 LOTTIE. Thanks for the personality assessment, Vesta.
 VESTA. Sure.

(A pause. MAMAW enters with TOMMY in tow. TOMMY still holds his comic books, sees everyone ... Hesitates.)

 TOMMY. I told Daddy. I hope you don't mind.
 MAMAW. Sit down, hon'. *(MAMAW leads him to the sofa. They sit.)* This is very important what we're going to talk about. A very important family meeting.
 TOMMY. I wish they didn't have to be here.
 MAMAW. Tommy, you can't live with me.

(TOMMY turns to LOTTIE.)

 TOMMY. You won't let me. I just hate you.
 LOTTIE. Tommy.
 MAMAW. It's not your mother. I won't let you.
 TOMMY. Why not?
 MAMAW. When I was a little girl I went with my momma up this back road ... it was clay ....
 TOMMY. Clay?
 MAMAW. There was an old woman that was dying. And, we were in this room of women talking, one had no teeth—said it was so hot the night before, she said, "I put the big *ban* in the big room and the little *ban* in the little room ...." Couldn't say "fan"—and we waited the longest time for the woman to die when someone said, "I think she's looking better."
 TOMMY. Better?
 MAMAW. And sure enough, the fever had broke and she woke up and everyone kinda got depressed. I heard her daughter say, "What are we going to do now?" See? They had come to bury her and she didn't die. They were looking to be free of her. They loved her but they wanted to get on with their own lives.
 TOMMY. Mamaw, you tell a story about practically everything

there is.

MAMAW. Tommy, hon', you have got to get out of this house and learn to live on your own. Papaw did you a disservice. He let you come here and keep him company but he didn't teach you anything.

TOMMY. Yes, he did.

MAMAW. No, he didn't.

TOMMY. Papaw was my best friend.

MAMAW. He was your friend but he shoulda been your granddad. Well, Papaw was selfish when it come to you. And I should have done something about that but I didn't. Papaw about wore me out taking care of him. But, son, you've about wore me out, too. 'Specially when you ask me the kinda questions you asked me today.

TOMMY. About having sex?

MAMAW. That's the one.

TOMMY. It's a good idea. Why can't we do it?

MAMAW. It's wrong. It's just about the wrongest thing I ever heard in my life. Tommy, don't you ever speak of it again because if you do I'll never speak to you again as long as I live. Now. Do you hear me?

TOMMY. I hear you, but ... why?

MAMAW. I don't want to be your girlfriend. I just don't want to.

TOMMY. But you said you love me, and I'm not supposed to want to live with you or for you to be my girlfriend or anything like that.

MAMAW. Yes.

TOMMY. And it's for my own good that I don't let any of those things be a part of what I want. So, I give up on all of that. But, can't I please stay with you?

MAMAW. No.

TOMMY. But what's going to happen to me?

LOTTIE. Let's go, Tommy.

(TOMMY stands.)

    TOMMY. No!
    DON. Tommy ....
    MAMAW. Go on!

THE PARKER FAMILY CIRCUS

TOMMY. You never answered my question!
MAMAW. Yes, I did.
TOMMY. No you didn't. WHAT'S GOING TO HAPPEN TO ME?

(TOMMY throws his comics. He rips one completely apart. DON moves to stop his son.)

DON. Son, no, NO! NO!!!

(Defiant, TOMMY turns over furniture. Rips the new slip covers from the sofa. Moves to the television.)

TOMMY. WHAT'S GOING TO HAPPEN TO ME? *(Looking for an answer. No one speaks.)* WHAT'S GOING TO HAPPEN TO ME? *(Before his father can reach him, TOMMY pulls the console TV on its face. TOMMY collapses in hysteria.)* WHAT'S GOING TO HAPPEN TO ME?

(DON and LOTTIE move to their son.)

POLLY. How could you do that? Mamaw, how could you when he loves you so much?
DON. Polly! Hush up!
POLLY. But he didn't mean it. He would never hurt you!
DON. Polly, that's enough!

(POLLY exits in tears. VESTA runs after her. LOTTIE and DON look to each other. They look to MAMAW for assistance. MAMAW turns away, disconnects.
LOTTIE tries to touch TOMMY. He pulls away. DON reaches him. He pulls away again. They kneel, grab him. He struggles. The parents surround him, overpowering his weakening resistance and clasp their son against them. TOMMY allows his mother to cradle and soothe him.)

TOMMY. Mama! I don't want to ....

LOTTIE. *(Whispers.)* Red Rover, Red Rover ... let Tommy come over....

MAMAW. Lottie, I'm going to put this house up for sale. I'm tired of taking care of it. I'm going to take me an apartment and I'm going to travel....

(TOMMY struggles to go to his grandmother. His parents restrain him.)

TOMMY. ... Mamaw, I'll come with you.

MAMAW. No, you can't. I'll come visit you at the new house so we'll still see one another, but ... well, it's for your own good.

TOMMY. But what's going to happen to me?

MAMAW. The same thing that happens to any of us. The sun shines, the sun sets, the moon comes up and goes down.

(TOMMY lunges forward again. His parents hold him.)

TOMMY. Mamaw, please ... don't do this.
MAMAW. I've got to, hon'.

(TOMMY gives up. LOTTIE releases him, wipes back his tears.)

LOTTIE. Tommy. It's all right. Come on. It's been a hard day.
MAMAW. He's a sweet boy, now.

(LOTTIE and DON help TOMMY to his feet.)

DON. Let's go home.

(TOMMY throws himself into his mother's arms, sobbing. LOTTIE realizes the full burden of her son is on her. She holds TOMMY tightly and then helps him from the room. Alone, DON speaks to his mother.)

DON. I know Cory was the colorful one in this house, and Papaw was the best electrician, better than all of us—but, I love you, Mama, and Lottie loves you. Like it or not, Cory's in prison and Papaw's dead, so we're about all that's left of the Parker family.

(DON exits. A beat. MAMAW rises wearily and picks up one of Tommy's mangled comic books. VESTA appears at the door.)

    VESTA. So, Mrs. Parker.
    MAMAW. Goodness, me. What are you still doing here?
    VESTA. You were awesome ... do you like need some help?
    MAMAW. No, you go on, hon'.
    VESTA. Ok, if you're sure.

(A beat.)

    MAMAW. Vesta?
    VESTA. Yes, ma'am?
    MAMAW. Do you want to go off to Austin?
    VESTA. Well, I guess so.... I don't have a choice, really ... because of my stepdaddy and, you know, things ....
    MAMAW. You'll do fine.
    VESTA. Yeah. OK, so ... if you go to Nicaragua?
    MAMAW. Yes.
    VESTA. Could you bring back a couple of boxes of cigars? I'll pay you.
    MAMAW. Oh, no. I don't believe you kids should be using tobacco.
    VESTA. Not to smoke, to sell. It's to sell.
    MAMAW. Get on ... get home. *(VESTA exits. MAMAW sits in Papaw's chair, holding the comic book to her. She glances at the fallen TV.)* Just get on to your own house. This is my house for as long as I'm here. Mine to do with as I see fit. Mine to sit here by myself ... if I could just press my lips against the back of your neck ... oh, Papaw.

THE END

COSTUME PLOT

MAMAW

beige knit slacks
floral print blouse
blue sweater
"Strides" shoes
eyeglasses on a chain
print apron w/pockets
hanging on coat rack: crocheted sweater
on hall table: handbag

TOMMY

cargo pants
cartoon t-shirt
hooded, zip front jacket
sneakers

POLLY

plaid skirt
button front blouse
dark tights
black maryjanes
denim backpack

VESTA

black studded short shorts
leather zip-front bustier
jeans jacket
red fishnet tights
Doc Martins
nose ring

LOTTIE

brown wool skirt
cream silk sweater
silk scarf
brown leather pumps
Coach bag
gold bracelet
wedding ring/engagement ring

DON

cargo work pants
thermal knit shirt
twill work shirt
wedding ring
yellow buck work boots

THE PARKER FAMILY CIRCUS

PROP LIST

ACT I

MAMAW

Scraps from slipcovers - preset on stage
Sewing basket and sewing supplies, straight pins
Cleaning cloth to clean sofa
1 set of keys - house/car
Reading glasses
Apron
Dish towel
Pots and pans - preset in kitchen
Purse
Lipstick

TOMMY

TV remote control - preset on stage
1 set of keys
Comic books

POLLY

Backpack
Watch

VESTA

Cell phone
Bag of potato chips
CD player, headphones
Backpack

LOTTIE

Cell phone
Pack of cigarettes
Purse

DON

Cell phone
Money
2 sets of keys: car keys and work keys
Watch

ACT II

TOMMY

Fake comic books

POLLY

Pie plate

VESTA

Pie plate

LOTTIE

Pie, peach cobbler - preset in kitchen, consumed onstage
Pie plate

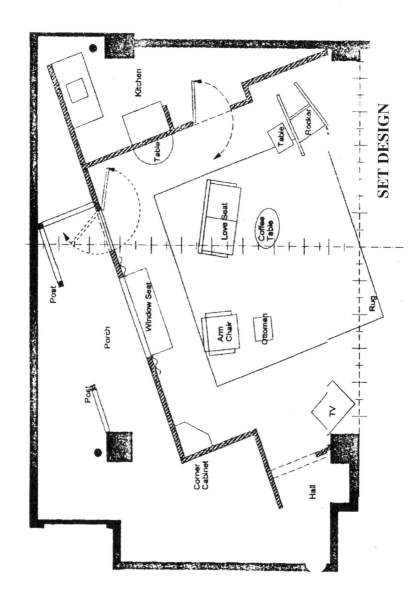